Bangkok, Thailand

Asian Travel Destination

Author
James Baker.

Publisher:
SONIT
2162 Davenport House, 261 Bolton Road. Bury. Lancashire. BL8 2NZ. United Kingdom.

Table of Content

Summary 1

Introduction to Bangkok 2

Physical and Human Geography 10

The landscape 10

Climate 10

The city layout 10

Traditional areas 11

Housing 12

The people 13

The economy 14

Industry 14

Finance 15

Transportation 15

Administration and social conditions 17

Government 17

Public utilities 17

Health 18

Education 18

Cultural life 19

History 22

Travel and Tourism 27

Bangkok Guide 27

Climate 27

Getting in 29

Getting around 53

Seeing 73

Doing 76

Eat 99

Drink 106

Sleep 110

Stay safe 112

Contact 122

Cope 124

Top things to do in Bangkok 128

The Grand Palace in Bangkok 128

Wat Arun in Bangkok 132

Bangkok Floating Markets 134

Khlong Lat Mayom Floating Market 134

Damnoen Saduak Floating Marke 137
Amphawa Floating Market 139
Chinatown Bangkok 142
Best Restaurants in Bangkok Chinatown 143
Lek & Rut Seafood in Chinatown 143
T & K Seafood 146
Cotton Restaurant at Shanghai Mansion Hotel 146
Krua Porn Lamai..149
Kuay Jab Nai Huan...150
Odean Crab Noodle Soup 150
Jok Kitchen...151
Raan Look Khing and other sweets carts...........................153
Hua Seng Hong..154
Himali Cha Cha..155
Shopping in Chinatown..155
Sampeng Lane Market 156
The Old Siam Plaza..158
Itsaraphap Lane 160
Nightingale-Olympic: Bangkok's Strangest Mall 160
Flashlight Market (Khlong Thom)......................................162
Little India Bangkok...163
Phahurat Shopping...165
Saphan Lek Market 165
Bangkok Museums...166
Bangkok National Museum 166
Museum of Siam...168
Moca - Museum of Contemporary Art Bangkok.....................171
Bangkokian Museum 174
Vimanmek Mansion in Bangkok 176

Summary

Traveling and Tourism

Tourism is a global industry, which involves people travelling across the world for a variety of reasons mainly recreation and sightseeing. When tourists decide where to travel, they often base their decisions on the attractions and situations in a city or country. Sometimes countries are in the midst of political unrest, such as war, civil war or terrorism. Tourists will avoid these destinations, choosing more peaceful destinations instead. However, while they are there, unforeseen situations may occur, such as tsunamis, natural disasters, diseases or accidents. It is important for tourism professionals and for tourists themselves to adequately prepare, through thorough research, before they (or their clients) leave on a journey.

Every country has sights of attractions and places of interest, some of which are not known that easy, and to discover them, you have to need a guide on the interested place, learn about local people's attitude and relation with foreginers, it is important to know all these. This is the importance of Tourist Book Guide

Introduction to Bangkok

A lot of first time visitors aren't quite sure what to expect when first arriving in the capital of exotic Thailand, and some may be disappointed by their first impressions on the way into town - endless high rise buildings, busy expressway flyovers and billboards of western companies advertising in English. Yet while Bangkok has undoubtedly embraced westernization and modernization, you only need to look a little under the surface to see that it remains undeniably a Thai place at heart.

In between the skyscrapers and sophisticated shopping centers there's still the remarkable Wat Phra Kaew and the Grand Palace, the Temple of the Dawn and many more. Traditions live on too: don't be surprised, for example, to find a large dedicated spirit house built for good luck alongside almost every major building, or to see files of Buddhist monks making their early morning alms round - and it's surely one of the only major cities in the world where seeing an elephant paraded round the streets hardly even ranks as being unusual.

What's wrong with Bangkok?

Amidst all of this lies one of Asia's most interesting and exciting cities, but it does have it's fair share of problems also - not least of which is the heat. Due to it's location in the tropics, Bangkok's average day time temperature is rarely much below 30 degrees centigrade at any time of year and the night time temperature is not much cooler. The maximum temperature can occasionally top 40 degrees during the hot season in April / May, when it is, not surprisingly, the low season for tourism. Despite the temperature, it is not all that sunny in Bangkok and most days are grey and overcast - meaning many visitors are surprised when they first walk outside Bangkok airport and discover that what appeared to be a cold, cloudy day is actually uncomfortably hot.

The heat, combined with the humidity and pollution, makes walking a sizable distance in Bangkok almost impossible, and breaking into a sweat after only a couple of hundred meters almost inevitable. The Thai people themselves will rarely walk any significant distance and there's a very large number of cars, buses,taxis and tuk-tuks to help them get about.

Sadly, these combine to make the traffic jams and pollution that Bangkok is justifiably world famous for. The seemingly permanent rot dtit (traffic jam) is a fact of life in Bangkok, and makes simple journeys that should take 20 minutes end up over an hour, even out of rush hour. The relatively small number of roads, the annual floods in September and October, and the hundreds of new cars flooding on to the roads every day don't help matters much either. However, Bangkok's impressive skytrain and new subway facilities combined now cover much of areas of the city a visitor is likely to go to and provide a convenient way to bypass them. Traffic jams in Bangkok

The combined effect of the traffic, heat, humidity, noise, dirt, pollution and the unappealing look of the city makes some want to leave Bangkok almost as soon as they've arrived. Though this is understandable to an extent, Bangkok has a lot to offer those who persevere.

The City of Angels

Despite all the problems, there's much to appreciate in Bangkok for those who persevere past negative first impressions and take the time to see it's attractions. Few of the Thais living in the city would want to forego the opportunities it offers and live elsewhere and for every foreigner who wants to leave as soon as possible, there's another who falls in love with it. The attractions are obvious: the impressive temples and tourist attractions, an endless number of decent restaurants, with food often at bargain prices (a ordinary meal and soft drink at a typical Thai restaurant may only you set you back around 40B (1 US$), and perhaps around 100 to 150B at a tourist orientated restaurant - though it is, of course, possible to pay much more). And wherever you are in the city, you will rarely have to walk more than 100m to find something to eat.

Getting about the city might be slow going due to all the traffic, but at least it's cheap and there's plenty of options. There is a comprehensive bus service that will take you all over the city in varying degrees of comfort, but the price is never more than about 25B (0.6 US$), and can be only 3.5 baht (0.1 US$) on the ordinary buses. Even when going from one side of central Bangkok to another, a taxi fare is rarely above 120B (3 US$), the only real exception being the journey to and from the airport. The skytrain was finished in December 1999, and for the areas it goes to, makes getting about quick and easy (although not particularly cheap compared to the taxis and buses). There are canal and river boats that effectively act as buses on the waterways, which are also very cheap and fast. The Khlong Saen Saep canal boats, in particular, are sadly underused by tourists as they provide a very quick and useful service, right across the city from Sukhumvit to Siam Square to Banglamphu for just a few baht. More transport schemes, including expansion of the the skytrain and subway lines, are underway too with notional completion dates in the next few years.

Shopping is also good value, with a huge variety of goods sold everywhere from street market stalls to upmarket in shopping centers. Shops are open every day, generally until around 9 or 10pm, which is convenient and makes it easy to get what you want, when you want it.

It's a great city for nightlife too, with an massive selection of pubs, bars and nightclubs, along with the famous adult-orientated entertainment. Bangkok also benefits from being, arguably, one of South East Asia's two most important cities (with Singapore). If there's an international cultural or social event going on in the region, chances are it's coming to Bangkok too.

And perhaps most importantly, there's the Thai people themselves who are surely some of the most friendly of any major capital city in the world. They seem remarkably tolerant of the challenges of life in the capital, and still manage to keep their fun loving and easy-going spirit. Try and emulate their jai yen (keeping your cool), a love of sanuk (having fun) and a feeling of mai pen rai (it doesn't matter, it's not important), and it will help you get the most from Bangkok. Those who take the time to see what it has to offer tend to be rewarded in Bangkok, while those who spend a couple of days there are likely to only get frustrated with the difficulties.

Finding your way around

Bangkok is split in two by the Chao Phraya river (the 'River of Kings', as it is sometimes translated). Almost all the tourists who come to Bangkok stay on the east side of the river, where the heart of the city is located. On the eastern side, between the river and the railway line is the where most of Bangkok's historic and impressive sights are, and if you have only 1 or 2 days in the capital, this the area to see. The Old

City area, known as Ko Rattanakosin, has the best including the Grand Palace and Wat Phra Kaew, Wat Pho, and the National Museum.

A little south of Banglamphu is the densely populated, noisy and busy Chinatown, orientated round Charoen Krung, Yaowarat road and Sampeng Lane. This areas contains the main train station (Hualamphong), and has consistently bad traffic jams, even by Bangkok's standards. Little India is adjacent to Chinatown, in the area around Pahurat and Chakraphet roads. This is perhaps the best place in the city for tailors, clothes are cheap and the range is huge.

Southeast of Chinatown are Sathorn and Bangrak districts, which consists of the area around Silom, Surawong, Sathorn and Si Phraya roads. This is the major financial and commercial district of the city, and also the original tourist area. Located by the river are some of Bangkok's oldest and finest hotels, such as The Oriental, Shangri-La, and Royal Orchid Sheraton. As a business district there are no sights around here as such, and traffic congestion is almost constant. There are however many middle to high end hotels, restaurants, shopping arcades and the (in)famous Patpong nightlife area. North of Silom is the Siam Square area (known as Pathumwan). This contains Chulalongkorn University, considered Thailand's top university, the National stadium, the ultra-modern shopping area of Siam Square and the many nearby shopping malls. The area is orientated mainly around Ploenchit road, which runs west to become Rama I road, and east to become Sukhumvit road. Like Silom, it has few sights as such, but many top hotels, such as the Hilton International Bangkok and Regent Bangkok, are here. The busy and noisy Pratunam district lies north of Pathumwan.

The 6 - 8 lane Sukhumvit road runs southeast from Ploenchit road. Once considered as on the outskirts of Bangkok, this has developed into the leading area for moderate hotels, and much of the lower end is crammed full of tourist facilities, including restaurants, shopping centers, and the Nana Plaza adult entertainment center. There are no sights here otherwise, and it takes a long time to get to the sights of Ko Rattanakosin. The lower end of Sukhumvit road (between soi 1 and 21) is very touristy, but it becomes a lot less so further up. The higher numbered sois are a popular residential area for foreign expats. Further down still, around Sukhumvit soi 71, is the area known as Phrakhanong which is also a good place for shopping, though it is not much visited by foreigners. Din Daeng, Bangkapi and Lat Phrao districts all lie to the north east of Sukhumvit, and are primarily residential areas. South of Sukhumvit is the port district of Khlong Toey, one of Bangkok's poorest areas that is generally best avoided.

The very large Thonburi district encompasses all of the areas west of the Chao Phraya river from Ko Rattanakosin, Chinatown etc...It's size and history (as the capital before Bangkok) give it a status of more than just a district of Bangkok. Charan Sanitwong road is the main aretry in Thonburi, running most of the way from north to south. Phra Pin Klao district is across the river from Banglamphu and this is now a good area for cheap shopping, with many markets and malls and reasonable nightlife. Somewhat confusingly for the foreigner, Bangkok Noi and Bangkok Yai districts are also in Thonburi, not in Bangkok proper across the river.

Bangkok is decentralized to a much greater degree than western cities, and it makes identifying the city center a tricky task. Perhaps the most commonly accepted area is the Siam Square area, but it could also be thought of as the Silom road district or the Ratchaprasong area. No area is really dominant, and you can be confident that wherever you are there will be huge shopping malls, restaurants and the like nearby.

Physical and Human Geography

The landscape

Climate

The climate of Bangkok is hot throughout the year, ranging from 77 °F (25 °C) in the "cold" season in December to 86 °F (30 °C) at the height of the hot season in April. The mean annual rainfall totals 60 inches (1,500 mm), four-fifths of which falls in brief torrential downpours during the late afternoons of the rainy season, which lasts from mid-May through September; the dry season lasts from December to February. Mean monthly relative humidity varies from a low of 60 percent in the cold season to more than 80 percent during the rainy season.

The city layout

Modern Bangkok has undergone explosive growth, which the authorities have attempted to direct by means of a series of master plans since the 1960s. The city centre, formerly enclosed by a wall, has long been densely developed. Later expansion has sprawled outward well beyond the administrative boundaries into the surrounding agricultural areas. Some districts have evolved into functional units as the inner city has become more institutional and commercial and the outer city more residential and industrial. Throughout the city, walled Buddhist temples and monasteries called wats, often sumptuously ornamented, serve as focal points for religious, cultural, and even commercial life.

Traditional areas

The governmental and commercial districts of the city occupy traditional sites. Government offices were originally housed in the walled compound of the 18th-century Grand Palace, but by the late 19th century they occupied surrounding palaces and mansions. The bureaucracy then spread outward into nearby colonial-style or Thai-style office buildings and homes along Ratchadamnoen Road. Multistoried buildings have been erected to meet the ever-increasing demand for space, and the traditional government compounds have become overbuilt. A number of large camps around and north of the National Assembly Hall constitute the military area.

When Bangkok became the national capital in the 18th century and its citadel was moved to the east bank of the Chao Phraya River, Chinese merchants and tradesmen occupying the site moved a short distance southward to the area now known as Sam Peng. Business was at first carried on in one-story wood and thatch houses. By the early 1900s a number of streets had been lined with two-story masonry shop-houses. This ever-expanding district now contains rows of shop-houses that are sometimes five or more stories high. Warehouses line both banks of the river just south of Sam Peng, while industry is concentrated at Sam Rong, south of the port. Nightlife flourishes on Pat Pong Road. The financial district straddles Silom Road.

In the Floating Market a variety of foods and merchandise are sold daily from boats on the canals near Wat Sai. Formerly several such markets and innumerable door-to-door floating vendors served the daily needs of the city's residents.

Housing

Homes generally consist of small, detached one- or two-story wooden houses or row houses. Most of these are overcrowded because there are far too few of them to house the expanding population. Government programs alone are insufficient to meet the housing shortage, and funds from the World Bank have been used to build low-income housing, such as the Din Daeng and Hua Mak developments. The government allows squatters to occupy unused public land. The number of squatters is small, and most of them are concentrated in the Khlong Toei area near the port.

Beginning in the 1960s, housing developed rapidly in the city. From the mid-1970s to the mid-1980s more than 100,000 new units were built. There was also an emphasis on renewal in inner-city areas. Private real-estate developers provide homes for middle-income groups, and many government agencies provide homes for their employees. Homes may be crowded onto small lots with rudimentary sanitation facilities. These developments have spread out haphazardly on the periphery of the city.

Luxury housing, mostly for the wealthy foreign community, usually takes the form of large, modern, two-story masonry structures set in private compounds and equipped with separate servants' quarters and kitchens. Bang Kapi is perhaps the most affluent neighbourhood. High-rise offices, hotels, and condominiums are increasingly common.

The people

The population's outstanding demographic characteristics its youth and the low proportion of non-Thais are explained by the high rate of natural increase and by the restrictive foreign immigration quotas adopted after World War II. Roughly two-fifths of the residents are under 20 years of age. The birth rate has declined since the introduction of a birth control program. At the same time, the net in-migration of young adults, particularly females, has increased greatly, so that more than a quarter of the resident population of the city is made up of migrant Thais from all parts of the country.

Most of the city's population are ethnic Thais. The Chinese are by far the largest minority, but there are sizable communities of other Asians, North Americans, and Europeans. Despite their small size, the foreign communities tend to live in certain areas. The Chinese concentrate in the commercial area of Sam Peng, Indians gather around mosques in the Wang Burapha section, and the Western and Japanese communities reside in the affluent, modern eastern section of the city.

Of the foreign groups, the Chinese enter the most intimately into city life. They appear to assimilate readily, and intermarriage is frequent. Their offspring are Thai citizens, and many Chinese families take Thai surnames and are naturalized.

The economy

Industry

There are many factories in the metropolitan area, but most operate on a small scale. Larger plants are located in the vicinity of the port, near the warehouses that store imported materials. Manufacturing is chiefly confined to food processing, textiles, the assembly of electronic equipment, and the production of building materials. Beginning in the mid-1970s, the government emphasized reducing congestion in the city and placed a high priority on locating industrial parks on the fringes of Bangkok. Roughly one-third of the country's output is produced in the city, and nearly half of all firms are located in the metropolitan area. Tourism has increased greatly and is now a major source of revenue in Bangkok.

Finance

Bangkok houses about one-third of the country's banking units, holding three-fourths of all deposits. The Industrial Finance Corporation of Thailand, the Board of Investment, and the Securities Exchange of Thailand are also located in the city.

Transportation

Bangkok's transportation system was originally based on water travel. The city's maze of canals connected with the river earned it the name "Venice of the East." The advent of the automobile, however, brought drastic changes. The number of vehicles in the city (including three-wheeled taxis, private cars, and buses colour-coded according to the region of service) increased, and a shortage of road space developed. The problem was met first by filling in most of the smaller and a number of the larger canals. This proved to be more than an aesthetic loss, however, because the waterway system had served to drain the waterlogged delta; flooding of the lower-lying parts of the city thus became increasingly frequent. Furthermore, the measure did not solve the problem of lack of space. Traffic became so congested that movement was increasingly difficult. To help ameliorate these problems, an authority was established in the 1970s to oversee bus transportation in the city, and in 1999 the city opened Skytrain, an elevated rail system.

Lines of communication radiate outward from the city. Roads run north to Laos and Chiang Mai, east to Kampuchea, and south to Malaysia. Railways run to the borders of Laos and Malaysia, to Chiang Mai in the north, and to Ubon Ratchathani and the Kampuchean border in the east. Bangkok International Airport is one of the busiest in Southeast Asia.

The port of Bangkok, located on the Chao Phraya River at Khlong Toei, is connected to the sea by a channel dug through the sandbar at the river mouth some 17 twisting miles (27 km) downstream. The port handles nearly all the nation's imports and exports.

Administration and social conditions

Government

The government of Bangkok Metropolis is administered by a governor and deputies. Developmental responsibilities rest with a large number of governmental agencies. Bangkok houses the headquarters of the United Nations Economic and Social Commission for Asia and the Pacific (ESCAP). In addition, the city houses various other UN agencies, including branch offices of the World Health Organization (WHO), the International Labour Organisation (ILO), the United Nations Children's Fund (UNICEF), and the International Bank for Reconstruction and Development (World Bank).

Public utilities

Most of the city's water supply comes from purification plants; it is drawn from the Chao Phraya and from deep wells. The pumping of water from wells has caused subsidence in parts of the city, which has increased flooding. Many people obtain water from polluted waterways. Sanitation facilities include sewers, storm drains, and the canals; some large buildings are equipped with septic tanks.

Bangkok consumes more than half of the country's electric power.

Health

Bangkok has most of the country's hospitals and clinics. Special services are offered for patients with tuberculosis and sexually transmitted diseases, and there are government homes for the indigent, handicapped, and aged. The Pasteur Institute and WHO supply vaccines. Family-planning clinics have proliferated in recent years. In the 1990s cases of AIDS increased among Bangkok's prostitutes and drug users. The government has established special wards in hospitals to treat patients afflicted with the disease and has taken other measures to prevent the spread of HIV infection.

Education

Because of its high proportion of school-age citizens, Bangkok's educational facilities are overburdened. There are too few schools, and the standard of instruction varies. Literacy is extremely high, however. Many of the government-built preprimary and primary schools are located on monastery grounds. Private primary and secondary schools run by foreign religious missions train the children of the elite. There are many private Chinese primary schools and night schools. The city has several universities. Wat Pho, long a traditional centre of learning, has often been considered the city's first university; it is one of the oldest and largest temples in Bangkok.

Cultural life

The most important cultural feature of Bangkok is the wat. There are more than 300 such temples, representing classic examples of Thai architecture. Most are enclosed by walls. Many wats have leased a portion of their grounds for residential or commercial use.

The National Museum houses prehistoric and Bronze Age art relics, as well as royal objects dating to the 6th century AD. The city also houses the National Library and the Thai National Documentation Department. Jim Thompson's Thai House, named for a U.S. entrepreneur and devotee of Thai culture, is composed of several traditional Thai mansions; it contains the country's largest collection of 17th-century Thai religious paintings. There are also collections of Dvaravati and Khmer sculpture, in addition to examples of Thai and Chinese pottery and porcelain. In 1987 the 200-acre (80-hectare) King Rama IX Royal Park with its extensive botanical gardens was opened to commemorate the king's 60th birthday.

All of the country's daily newspapers and most of its weeklies and monthlies are published in Bangkok. Newspapers are printed in Thai, English, and Chinese. Radio and television are controlled by government agencies and the military. Most of the nation's radio stations and all of its television stations are located in or near Bangkok. Most programs are in Thai, but some special programs are in English and Chinese. Motion pictures are extremely popular. There is a thriving Thai cinema industry, but films are also imported.

Fairs, festivals, and "kite-fighting" contests are held in the parks. The Ratchadamnoen and Lumphini stadiums host professional boxing bouts featuring the highly ritualistic form of boxing known as Muai Thai. Silapakorn National Theatre presents dancing, drama, and music.

In Thailand, all roads lead to Bangkok. The capital is the nation's political center, its spiritual and cultural hub, and a magnet for migrants from all over the country. The country is 95 percent Buddhist, and Bangkok is blessed with hundreds of temples, from humble pagodas to grand, gold-spired complexes. Thais do a fine job of balancing the spiritual and the earthly, however, and just as strong as these religious beliefs is the emphasis on sanuk, the idea that life should be fun.

Temples are an essential part of any itinerary, and it's important to be versed in some cultural etiquette before exploring them. The basic rule of thumb is to respect tradition and dress conservatively. You don't need head-to-toe formal clothing, but your shoulders and knees should be covered.

Traditional Thai festivals are a highlight for visitors to Bangkok. The river festival, Loy Krathong, takes place in the twelfth month of the Thai lunar calendar (it usually falls in November) and involves fireworks, lanterns, and thousands of floating offerings to the river spirits on the Chao Phraya river. Songkran, or Thai New Year, occurs in April and is a raucous celebration in which locals and visitors drench each other with water in the name of good fun

History

Bangkok became the capital of Siam (as Thailand was previously known) in 1782, when General Chao Phraya Chakkri, the founder of the ruling Chakkri dynasty, assumed the throne as Rama I and moved the court from the west to the east bank of the Chao Phraya River. The move appears to have been dictated by strategic considerations: the wide westward bend in the river constituted a wide moat guarding the northern, western, and southern perimeters of the new site. To the east stretched a vast, swampy delta called the Sea of Mud, which could be traversed only with extreme difficulty. Rama I modeled the new city on the former capital, Ayutthaya, 40 miles (64 km) to the north. By the end of his reign the city was established. The walled Grand Palace complex and the temple Wat Pho were completed. A new city wall, perhaps the most imposing structure, skirted the river and Khlong Ong Ang to the east; it was 4.5 miles (7 km) long, 10 feet (3 metres) thick, and 13 feet (4 metres) high, and it had 63 gates and 15 forts. The area enclosed amounted to 1.5 square miles (4 square km).

More wats were built during the reigns of Rama II (1809–24) and Rama III (1824–51). They served as schools, libraries, hospitals, and recreation areas, as well as religious centres. During these years Wat Arun, noted for its tall spire, Wat Yan Nawa, and Wat Bowon Niwet were completed, Wat Pho was further enlarged, and Wat Sutat was begun. There were, however, few other substantial buildings and fewer paved streets; the river and the network of interconnected canals served as roadways.

Rama IV (1851–68) developed the city while continuing, at a reduced rate, the traditional building of wats. The Grand Palace was improved, a number of substantial dwellings were constructed for members of the royal family, several new streets were laid down, and a reduction was made in the large number of floating houses anchored along the riverfront. A new route, Charoen Krung (New Road), leading southward, was constructed, and a new city moat, Khlong Phadung Krung Kasem, parallel to the city's first canal, was dug and fortified; a long canal led from it to the present port area (Khlong Toei), thus allowing small boats to bypass the large bend in the river immediately south of the city. A pony path, now a major highway, was laid atop the mud heaped up beside this waterway.

During the long reign of Rama V, King Chulalongkorn (1868–1910), the city was transformed through a program of public works. The great triple-spired Chakkri Building in the Grand Palace was completed by

1880. The Dusit Palace and an ancillary garden city were later built beyond the wall, being connected to the Grand Palace by the European-inspired Ratchadamnoen Nok Road. A road- and bridge-building program was embarked on in earnest, because King Chulalongkorn, an early automobile enthusiast, foresaw the effect that the motor vehicle would have on city development. Most of the now obsolete city wall was pulled down to build the roads, but two forts, a large gate, and a section of the wall were preserved. The centenary of the city, in 1882, was marked by the inauguration of many social reforms, manifested in the public buildings used for their administration, as well as by the completion of the great royal temple, Wat Phra Kaeo, which housed the Emerald Buddha. A post and telegraph service was organized in the 1880s, an electric tram service was instituted on Charoen Krung in 1892, and the first line of the State Railway, running from Bangkok to Phra Nakhon Si Ayutthaya, opened in 1900. Nor were aesthetic considerations forgotten, for other new buildings included the marble temple of Wat Benchamabopit (1900), elegant bridges in the French style, and the Italian-inspired National Assembly Hall (Throne Hall).

Rama VI (1910–25) continued the program of public works. He established Chulalongkorn University in 1916, built a system of locks to control the level of waterways throughout the city, and gave the public its first and largest recreational area Lumphini Park. During

Rama VII's reign (1925–35) municipal areas were delimited as part of a general administrative reorganization aimed at decentralization. In 1937 Bangkok was formally divided into the municipalities of Krung Thep and Thon Buri. At the time of their establishment, the two municipalities, approximately equal in area, together covered about 37 square miles (96 square km); about four-fifths of the city's population lived in Krung Thep.

Since World War II Bangkok has grown with unprecedented rapidity, which caused problems with transportation, communication, housing, water supply, drainage, and pollution. Tourism rose in importance during the Vietnam War, when the city became a popular destination for U.S. military personnel. By the 1980s, nightclubs and the tourist sex trade as well as crime and sexually transmitted diseases were flourishing. Although prostitution is formally illegal and the number of prostitutes per capita is lower in Thailand than in some other Asian countries, the city's commercial sex industry employs an estimated 100,000 people and is popular among foreign tourists. However, the vast majority of clients are Thai nationals. To combat abuses, notably underage prostitution, the government stiffened penalties for both patrons and brothel operators during the 1990s. That those responsible for modernizing the metropolis are coping with these problems suggests the appropriateness of its official emblem: the God Indra seated atop a sacred white elephant, the four tusks of which denote its celestial status and its ability to accomplish the impossible. Throughout the 1980s the city experienced an economic boom, which was blunted by an economic crisis that hit Asia in the late 1990s. However, the city continued its role as one of Asia's most important tourist, financial, and commercial centres. The city's uniquely Thai character, while perhaps diminishing, provides a vibrant backdrop for Bangkok's cosmopolitan image.

Travel and Tourism

Bangkok Guide

Climate

Climate	Jan	Feb	Mar	Apr	May	Jun	Jul	Aug	Sep	Oct	Nov	Dec
Daily highs (°C)	32	33	34	35	34	33	33	33	32	32	32	31
Nightly lows (°C)	21	23	25	26	26	25	25	25	25	24	23	21
Precipitation (mm)	9	29	28	64	220	149	154	196	344	241	48	9

Bangkok - Weather forecast

According to the World Meteorological Organization (WMO), Bangkok is one of the hottest cities in the world. Located just 14 degrees north of the Equator, Bangkok is warm at any time of the year with temperatures over 30°C (86°F).

The most pleasant time to visit is the cool season that lasts from November till February. It is both the coolest and driest period the

Emerald Buddha statue in Wat Phra Kaew even wears a scarf during this period! Don't think that's necessary though daytime temperatures still hover around 32°C (89.6°F), but it does cool down into the lower 20's as it gets dark (lower 70's °F). March and April represent the hot season, and hot it is 35°C (95°F) on average, but don't be surprised to see temperatures rising towards 40 degrees Celsius (around 100°F+). This is the worst season to visit Bangkok, so plan a lot of air-conditioned shopping mall visits and get a hotel with a swimming pool. Then there's the wet season that runs from May till October. Expect massive downpours resulting in floods all over the city, and spells of thunder at times. It's not all bad though the afternoon showers are actually a pleasant way to cool down from the heat, and while they may last all day, usually they're over within an hour. Extreme rainfall happens in September and October, so these months are best avoided.

Whatever season you're visiting, don't take the weather lightly temple-tramping in the scorching afternoon sun can be a challenge, so come well-prepared. Dress lightly for the weather, but keep in mind that some palaces and all temples (notably the Grand Palace) have a strict dress code. Also be sure, and this cannot be said enough, drink enough fluids! You don't have a reason not to, as 7-Elevens and other convenience stores are abundant in Bangkok and they sell cooled beverages for as little as 10 baht. Locals get their water from "reverse osmosis" purified water machines that fill up a one litre bottle for one baht

Getting in

Getting in by plane

Bangkok is served by two airports: Suvarnabhumi Airport and Don Muang Airport. Suvarnabhumi Airport is used by all airlines in Thailand except for Nok Air, Orient Thai and Air Asia, which use the old Don Muang Airport. Both these airports are about 30 km (19 mi) from the city centre, so be prepared for a long ride to get into the city. Also allow *at least* three hours to connect between them, as they are far away from each other and there is heavy congestion on the roads. However, if you arrive at one of these and have a flight within a few hours from the other, then there is a free shuttle bus service which uses the tollways. You need to show your ticket to get on board.

Suvarnabhumi Airport

Located 30km (19 mi) to the east of Bangkok (in the Samut Prakan province), space-age Suvarnabhumi Airport, pronounced "soo-wanna-poom") (IATA: BKK) started operations in Sep 2006 and is now Bangkok's main airport and the busiest airport in Southeast Asia. It is used for almost all international and domestic flights to Bangkok. There is only one terminal building, which covers both domestic and international flights, but it is *huge* (by some measures the world's largest), so allow time for getting around. There are two immigration sections, but processing time can be lengthy 30 minutes and more.

Facilities

Suvarnabhumi offers all facilities you would expect from a major international airport. There's a transit hotel, ATMs, money exchange, restaurants, tax-free shops, an observation lounge and even a "redemption booth", very reassuring for karmically challenged passengers. There are about 50 dining venues spread over the terminal building. The one that sounds most interesting probably is Panda Ready To Eat, but the cheapest place for a meal is Magic Food Point on level 1, near gate 8. There are a few stores in the check-in area, including a convenience store and a post office; however, the real shopping experience awaits visitors on the other side of immigration in the departure area, where the number of shops and duty free outlets leaves you wondering whether you are in an airport or a mall. There is not much to see at the observation deck on the seventh floor, since the steel structure of the roof blocks most of the view.

> ➤ The duty free shops offer a wide range of almost every international brand. The prices are not competitive.

> ➤ Beware of buying at airport convenience stores, located before security, if you are to bring those items inside. All cans and

bottles (even containing food) are confiscated by security at check-in.

➢ Currency exchange options are abundant, but virtually all offer a dearer exchange rate than downtown. A much better rate is normally available from the red booth near the coin ticket kiosks for the Airport Express Line (right after entrance to the Airport Express Line).

➢ Free Wi-Fi for up to one hour is available in the departure lounge, after security and passport control; the login details can be obtained from the Information point. Access can be frustratingly unstable and unreliable.

➢ If you need a hard copy of maps and brochures you can go to the Tourism Authority of Thailand (TAT) booth at Suvarnabhumi Airport: Arrival Floor, International Tel: (66)2134 0041 Open 24 hours Suvarnabhumi Airport Arrival Floor, Domestic Tel: (66)2134 0040 Open 24 hours

Transport

➢ There are plenty of ways to get into the city from Suvarnabhumi Airport. Most people opt for the Airport Rail Link, by far the fastest way to get into downtown, although taxis are also reasonably priced by world standards.

> Located on the basement level of the passenger terminal, the Airport Rail Link

City Line is a commuter rail line that stops at all stations. Trains leave every 15min, and after Makkasan station it continues to Ratchaprarop and Phaya Thai stations. The ride to Phaya Thai takes 24min from/to the airport and costs 45 baht. (the ride to or from Makkasan is 35 baht, Ratchaprarop is 40 baht, Lat Krabang is 15 baht). They run from 0600 to 2359.

If you're heading downtown, the Airport Rail Link has a good connection to the BTS Skytrain at Phaya Thai, though you will have to buy a new ticket. If Khao San Road is your final destination, you can hail taxis from the main road (around 60 baht, c. 6km distance), or hop aboard bus **15** (7 baht); this bus leaves from across Central World, BTS Siam, and BTS National Stadium and goes along Ratchadamnoen Klang Road and Chakrabongse Road serving both sides of Khao San Road.

Getting in by Buses
There are free shuttle buses from Suvarnabhumi Airport to Don Muang Airport every hour between 05:00-23:00. You have to show them your flight ticket to board. At Suvarnabhumi Airport, get on the bus at gate 2 or 3. At Don Muang Airport, get on the bus at the ground floor arrival terminal. The shuttle bus goes directly via the express way, and does not stop during the ride.

Private Airport Express buses, including backpacker favourite AE2 to Khao San Road, stopped running in Jun 2011. Recenkly a new bus service called S1 started to operate from BKK aiport to the junction between khao san and rambuttri streets. Tickets are 60 baht per person, busses depart from level 1 of the airport, outside gate 7 and go every 30 minutes or so between 06:00 and 22:00.

To take a public bus or minibus, you must first take the free shuttle bus from outside the second floor, gate 5 to the Public Transportation Center a few kilometres away. From there, The BMTA public bus lines are:

➢ 550: Suvarnabhumi to Bang Kapi

➢ 553: Suvarnabhumi to Samut Prakan

➢ 554: Suvarnabhumi to Don Muang Airport

➢ 555: Suvarnabhumi to Rangsit (using the expressway)

➢ 558: Suvarnabhumi to Central Rama 2

Note that almost all of the routes were already suspended, leaving 5 routes that link to non-touristy places except 554. (Source: local)

These services take about 1-2 hours depending on traffic; frequency is usually every 20min during daytime. At night, it ranges from 20 minutes to one hour depending on the route. There are also privately-owned BMTA minibuses to many parts of Greater Bangkok, such as

Don Muang Airport, Bang Kapi, Rangsit and Samut Prakan. They charge a flat rate of 50 baht and go directly to the destination, so they are faster than public buses that stop frequently along the way. To get to Khao San Road take Airport Rail Link City Line to Makkasan (35 baht) and change there to bus number 556 (13 baht), which will take you next to Democracy Monument from where it's a short walk to Khao San Road.

These buses are not very frequent so prepare for as much as 30-40 min waiting time. This is probably the cheapest possible way how to get from/to airport for 48 baht total. (The 556 bus goes on from Democracy Monument to Southern Bus Terminal- Sai Tai.) Though you could take bus 554 to Synphaet Hospital and then public bus 60 or alternatively bus 555 to Din-Daeng Road followed by bus 171, both options will take you through heavy Bangkok traffic on normal roads with frequent stops, thus making the Airport Link the best and fastest option.

Long-distance first class bus services connect Suvarnabhumi Airport directly with Chachoengsao, Nong Khai, Pattaya, Rayong, and Trat.

Taxis
Top-level egress to queueless taxis

Ordinary metered taxis are available on the first floor (one floor below arrivals). Follow the "public taxi" signs that lead to the outside of the airport premises, queue up and state your destination at the desk

(English is understood). Once there was a desk and you got a card ticket with two sections - one to give to the driver, often with your destination written in Thai - The small part for you was for complaints and is how the system is enforced: hold on to it to help avoid arguments later. Now queue tickets are dispensed by machine at the head of the two snake queues. There is a 50 baht surcharge on top of the meter (*not* per passenger!), meaning that trips to the city will cost 250-400 baht (plus possible expressway tolls of 50 and 25 baht, depending on time). Make sure you have change ready to pass to the toll operators to avoid being overcharged for the tolls later on.

With very smooth traffic (which rarely occurs other than say in the wee hours), the ride takes about 30 minutes and costs under 250 baht (excluding tolls and surcharges). Otherwise, count on it taking 45-60 minutes and closer to 300 baht (excluding tolls and surcharges). During rush hour it can take much longer. No other surcharges apply, not even for going back to the airport. If there is a huge taxi queue, consider taking a limousine taxi, or take the free shuttle bus to the Public Transport Centre, which has more taxis. Go straight to the "official public taxi stand" and wait there. It is rare, but there have been reports of rigged meters that make the ride cost more than 400 baht. These taxis usually appear highly modified and it is a good idea to avoid them, or record the licence plate number of the taxi.

You should also watch out for 'helpful' touts hovering nearby the main taxi desk who will lead you across the road to legitimate taxis. These drivers will refuse to use the meter by saying there is heavy traffic and will charge a phenomenal price supposedly based on distance and number of passengers - for instance, they will quite brazenly tell you it will cost 2,500 baht to take two people to the city centre. Refuse to deal with these touts on sight. However, should you make the mistake of trusting them, find out the fare before they have a chance to leave the airport. Quoting the correct metered price (250-400 baht, as above) will garner a response that you'll need to take a bus to get that kind of price. Stand your ground and insist they take you back to the airport - provided you do this before you leave, they'll be quite happy to take you back with no charge.

So-called limousine taxis (which charge by distance, eg, around 800 baht to Sukhumvit) can be reserved at the limousine hire counter on the second floor (just outside arrivals), and aggressive touts will try to entice you on board. If you allow yourself to be waylaid by one of these taxi touts, they might quote you more than double the fare than an ordinary metered taxi would charge (900 baht instead of 400 baht, for example). You'd be silly even acknowledging their existence ignore and walk straight past them.

Accommodation near the airport

There are plenty of hotels near Suvarnabhumi Airport, and huge construction projects are planned for the future. Day room facilities for transit passengers are now available at the Miracle Grand Louis Tavern on floor 4, concourse G, +66 2 134-6565, 2,000 baht per 4-hour block, no reservations accepted. Travellers looking for a free quiet place to doze undisturbed at night can use one of the benches on the bottom floor of the terminal (which seem to be a popular choice with tourists and locals).

All other accommodation in Bangkok is listed in the relevant district articles. If you want an overnight stay within 20min of the airport, get a hotel along Lat Krabang Road, here covered in the Lat Krabang district. The Tourist Authority of Thailand and other hotel and tourist agencies have counters on the arrivals floor of the main terminal. You can make reservations at plenty of hotels here. Check for special promotions and also whether the hotel offers an airport pick-up and drop-off service especially useful for late night arrivals and early morning departures.

Don Muang Airport
Don Muang Airport (IATA: DMK) (or Don Mueang), about 30 km (19 mi) north of downtown, was Bangkok's main airport until 2006. The airport currently handles Nok Air and Orient Thai domestic flights, the international terminal is now used by Air Asia and charters. Since 1 Oct 2012 all Air Asia flights arrive at and leave from DMK (Don Muang)

instead of BKK (Suvarnabhumi). This might be something to consider when you have a connecting flight, since most non-Air Asia international flights will be leaving from BKK (Suvarnabhumi).

Visa Photos are available at the business centre in the Amari Hotel. They charge 150 bath for six photos. To get there, use elevator located nearby exit number 6 and cross the bridge.

The public taxi stand is on the pavement outside the arrivals area (don't be fooled by all the taxi service booths in the main hall), and is probably your best bet for getting into town it's your only option after 23:00. A trip to MBK can cost roughly 250 baht depending on traffic. The same booth and slip system as at Suvarnabhumi Airport is used here. If the queue at the taxi stand is long or you need a more spacious car, you may want to book a (so-called) limousine taxi from the desks in the terminal. This will get you a slightly nicer car at about twice the price (500-600 baht). Ignore any touts outside and do not get into any car with white licence plates, as these are not licensed to carry passengers. If you are having trouble finding drivers willing to put the meter on, or want to avoid the airport taxis, you can walk to the main road outside by turning right outside the arrivals door and walking past the area where the buses are parked and make your way left towards the main road. You can hail down a taxi here, and the driver should put on the meter, this would be the cheapest fare.

Across a covered overpass from the airport is Don Muang Train Station. Tickets to Hualamphong Train Station in central Bangkok cost 20 baht at the ticket booth. Trip time to Hualamphong is at least 60 minutes. While taking the train is the cheapest way to get from the airport to Bangkok, it is not for the faint-of-heart: schedules are erratic, the run-down passenger cars often have beggars roaming through them, and are relatively empty late at night. Still if you board the train at Don Muang, you immediately plunge from the shiny world of airports that are virtually the same everywhere into a very Thai Thailand, and during the day it makes an interesting journey. If you have been on third class Thai trains before, this one is no different. On every train station, vendors board the train to supply you with food and drinks. Thais will smile at you as they will do during the rest of your holiday, pleased to see a "farang" (a Thai word derived from "foreigner").

It is not advisable to try to get to the Don Muang airport by train when you have a flight to catch - trains run with very little regard for the scheduled timetable, and it is not uncommon to arrive more than an hour past the expected time. Add an extra hour or two to your journey time if you intend to get to the airport this way. Trains regularly depart late from the train station and its journey is hampered by the fact that the train sometimes gives way to traffic at some level crossings. [Expect for the train to be at a halt for up to fifteen minutes at some junctions (Dec 2012)]. Despite all this, if you have hours to kill, it is a highly recommended journey to take, especially if you are running low on Thai Bhat, as the journey is an amazing 8 baht (Dec 2012).

There is also a free shuttle bus service between DMK and BKK Suvarnabhumi airport. At peak times, it runs every 30 min and it takes about an hour, depending on traffic. The signs to the bus stop aren't that good but to get to it, all you have to do is turn left once you come out of the terminal building (with the taxi queue behind you) and walk towards the end of the building / pavement. If you have time to spare, this is a cheap way of getting into town from DMK since Suvarnabhumi offers many transport options.

There are two airport bus lines at DMK operated by BMTA (orange aircon bus). The ticket is 30 baht. You can take bus just in front of the terminal. It makes good connection to the BTS Skytrain and MRT subway

A1 to BTS Mo Chit/MRT Chatuchak and Mo Chit 2 Intercity Bus Terminal and return. A2 (new) runs to BTS Mo Chit then Victory Monument and return.

There are also a number of public transport buses passing through the airport. Just follow the signs toward the bus stop. Airport to your back, the bus stop is on the right-hand side of the airport (ie, north of the airport). It will be along the highway, outside the airport complex, right below a highway footbridge. Buses towards central Bangkok are at the airport's side of the road, so don't cross the highway. These are useful bus lines:

➢ Air-conditioned bus 504 will take you to CentralWorld at Ratchaprasong intersection (close to Siam Square), as well as to Lumphini Park and Silom, from where you can have access to the Skytrain.

➢ Ordinary and air-conditioned bus 29 will take you to Hualamphong Train Station passing by many places, including Victory Monument and Siam Square. You can also get off at the Chatuchak Weekend Market, where you can switch onto the metro or Skytrain.

➢ Air-conditioned bus 59 will take you to Sanam Luang in Rattanakosin. This route is time-consuming as Rattanakosin is far off from the airport.

➢ Bus 510 to Victory Monument.

Keep in mind that some of these buses, especially air-conditioned bus 29, don't complete the route. They are called "additional bus" (Thai: รถเสริม rot serm). These kind of buses have a red sign in front of them with the final destination written on it (in Thai script of course). Check this before taking the bus. You can ask the locals at the bus stop or a conductor on the bus.

Passengers have reported difficulty with using some of these buses due to the scarcity of English-speaking conductors. Thus it is worthwhile to have your destination written down in Thai script and show it to the conductor, or even people at the bus stop, as this is a great help.

Airport Bus

> A1 DMK Mochit BTS/MRT (Chatuchak) Mochit 2 / Northeastern Bangkok Bus Station DMK

> A2 DMK Mochit BTS/MRT (Chatuchak) Saphan Kwai BTS Ari BTS Sanam Pao BTS Victory Monument DMK

Airport bus from the Don Muang airport services routes at a frequency of 20 minutes and each route takes about 60-80min per trip. The fare for airport bus is fixed at 30 baht per person per trip.

City Bus

> **Bus 29** DMK Laksi Mochit BTS/MRT (Chatuchak) Victory Monument Sam Yan Bangkok Railway Station

> **Bus 29** (air conditioned) - DMK Mochit BTS/MRT (Chatuchak) Victory Monument Sam Yan Bangkok Railway Station

> **Bus 510** - DMK Laksi Mochit BTS/MRT (Chatuchak) Saphan Khwai Victory Monument

> **Bus 555** - DMK Laksi Horwang Din Deang Praram 9 Suvarnabhumi Airport

➢ **Bus 59** - DMK Bangkhen Kasetsart University Central Lad Phrao Chatuchak Saphan Khwai Victory Monument Ratchadamnern Sanamlung (Khao San Road)

➢ **Bus 554** - DMK Laksi Ramintra Suvarnabhumi Airport

➢ **Bus 187** - DMK Din Daeng Ratwiti Victory Monument Charoenkrung Thanam Sipraya

➢ **Bus 538** - DMK Din Daeng Victory Monument Rama Hospital

➢ **Bus 504** - DMK Din Daeng Pratunam Silom Saphan Krung Thep

The fare for City bus is charged in the range of 6.5-23 baht depending on the route and type of bus taken.

By bus
When buying tickets for buses out of Bangkok, it's best to skip travel agents and their private buses, whose rates are a 50 to 100 percent premium over regular government rates, and get the bus tickets directly at Bangkok's three public bus terminals. These buses are much cheaper, generally safer, more comfortable and won't scam you onto a clapped-out minibus halfway along the way. Each of these long haul bus terminals serve a different direction. They are purposefully located in off-central locations, so the long-haul buses avoid the heavy traffic congestion in the centre of the city. Beware of the so-called tourist information booth on the second floor of Hua Lamphong train station, as that's a travel agency in disguise, offering overpriced bus

voyages to popular destinations around Thailand. They have been known to employ overly friendly persons in official-looking uniform to entice customers.

The largest, busiest, and most modern terminal is the Northern Bus Terminal, +66 2 936-2841(-3), also known as Mo Chit 2. The upper floor serves the Isaan region in the northeast of Thailand; the ground floor serves Northern Thailand, and shares some destinations with Ekkamai (including Pattaya, Rayong, Chanthaburi and Trat). The bus terminal is a fair hike from BTS station Mo Chit or MRT station Chatuchak Park. Motorbike taxis do the trip for a fixed 30 baht fare (bargaining is pointless), while tuk-tuks charge whatever they feel like when bargaining, remember that a real taxi with air-conditioning will cost you about 45 baht (assuming little traffic). You can also take bus 77 and pay the 13 baht fare on board (this bus also goes from the terminal via Victory Monument, Pratunam and Silom Road. If you have a considerable amount of luggage, the easiest, if not necessarily fastest, option is to take a taxi directly to or from the bus terminal.

Buying tickets here is reasonably easy; find a window with your destination written on it (in friendly Roman letters), pay the fare in big numbers on the same window, and you'll get a ticket on the next available departure. Note that blue writing means 1st class, red means 2nd class (avoid on longer trips), and tickets for destinations in Isaan are sold from the third floor. Ask the information desk on the first floor if you need help, or any of the BKS staff, easily identifiable thanks to their natty white shirts with gold buttons. Now just find the departure stall and you're on your way. If you have time to kill, there are two fairly decent air-conditioned food courts at both ends of the main terminal building, plus KFC, Dunkin' Donuts and lots of 7-Eleven outlets.

The Eastern Bus Terminal, +66 2 391-2504, also known as Ekkamai, is a relatively compact terminal right next to Ekkamai BTS station in Sukhumvit. Ekkamai serves destinations in Eastern Thailand, including Pattaya, Rayong, Ban Phe (for Ko Samet), Chanthaburi and Trat. If you're heading for Ko Chang, there is a specifically designated stop for it between Chanthaburi and Trat. You can also get a bus to the Cambodian border crossing at Poipet, look for the bus to Aranyaprathet and tell them you are going to Poipet when you buy the ticket.

Then there's the Southern Bus Terminal, +66 2 894-6122, also known as Sai Tai Mai, that serves all destinations west and south of Bangkok from its somewhat inconvenient location on the Thonburi side of the river. In December 2007, the terminal moved to a new, even more remote location, at Phutthamonthon Sai 1 Road in northern Thonburi. It is a 70 baht taxi ride to the Bank Khae area of Bangkok. Long-distance buses leave from here to destinations throughout Western Thailand (including Nakhon Pathom and Kanchanaburi) and Southern

Thailand (including Krabi, Phuket, Surat Thani, Ko Samui, Ko Pha Ngan, Hat Yai, and many others). It also has a huge number of minibuses out back which take trips to most of the places the buses go, and do it a lot quicker.

However, if you have large baggage, forget this option. The new terminal is a fairly pleasant airport-like structure with air-conditioning, electronic departure monitors (in English), a few bank offices, nice and cheap food. Unlike the rip-off operators at Khao San Road, all buses from here are public, well-regulated, cheap, and reasonably safe. Just buy your tickets at the numbered desk with your destination posted on it (almost always in English). There are also plenty of taxis out the back of the bus terminal.

Getting to the terminal is a bit of headache, as public transport is limited. The easiest option is to take a metered taxi, but if you're going there in the evening, especially during workdays, be prepared to fight a serious traffic jam getting there can take 30 minutes or an hour from the city centre. A taxi ride from Khao San Road should end up around 120 baht in favourable traffic conditions. Ignore touts unlike what they might say, there really is no "faster" way when all the roads are congested.

From Victory Monument BTS station, the terminal can be reached with pale orange air-conditioned bus 515 (17 baht). When approached by an on-board bus conductor, just say "Sai Tai". After quite a ride, the large bus terminal will be on the left side about 9 km after crossing the river (you won't miss it and probably will be told as well). Getting there by bus actually does not take much more time than taxi (it's almost the same in the likely case of a traffic jam), but the ride is much cheaper, especially if alone. Bus 556 no longer goes from Suvarnabhumi Airport, but from Makkasan Airport Rail Link (ARL) station. There are also white minibuses (30 baht) from various points around Bangkok, eg. from Ramkhamhaeng (near Rajamangala National Stadium). There are inexpensive shuttle buses and slightly more expensive (but quicker loading and a bit faster) minibuses to and from the Northern Bus Terminal as well. A meter-taxi from Northern Bus Terminal (Morchit) is about 150-180 Baht and takes about 30-50 minutes. Insist on the meter. There are plenty of taxis at the entrance of the big hall.

From the Hualamphong station, one can take the 507 (15 baht) non-airconditioned bus. It infrequently stops on the far side of the multi-road intersection from the front of the rail station and goes directly to the terminal. Allow 60-90min to wait for the bus and for the long distance and the traffic.

From the Khao San Road/Democracy Monument area, you can take the orange 511 (15 baht). The New Southern Bus Terminal is the last stop on the route.

By minibus

For travelling to Bangkok suburbs, the fastest and often the cheapest way is to use public minibus (minivan) services. They are running from the rear of the Victory Monument square (facing the monument itself are the city bus stops, behind it there is a small market, and behind the market you will find many white-coloured minibuses (13.76414N 100.53878E) just parking at the roadside and waiting for passengers). They depart when full, usually every 10-30 min. Fare is usually similar to long-distance buses with the same destination (if there are any). Other way, it could be estimated as 1 baht/km.

Please note that minibuses to the surrounding provinces have been moved from Victory Monument to the bus stations - Mo Chit, Tai Mai, and Ekkamai. (as at Nov 2016). The only ones from here now are to destinations within the Bangkok area, like Rangsit.

There are also plenty of minibuses at the Southern Bus Terminal, out the back. These go to various locations in the south and also within the city itself. There is one to Bang Phli,(in Samut Prakhan Province) from where buses/minibuses to Rayong/Pattaya can be found

By train
East Asia train travel map

The State Railway of Thailand, +66 2 222-0175, serves Bangkok with railway lines from all four directions of Thailand.

Hualamphong Train Station is the most important station, located close to Yaowaratand served by its own MRT station. It's a big and surprisingly convenient station built during the reign of King Rama VI. It was spared from bombing in World War II at the request of the Thai resistance movement.

Tickets for trains leaving the same or the next day can be bought on the counters under the big screens. The Advance Booking Office is located to the right of the platforms as you walk towards them and is quite well-organised. You can select your seat/berth from a plan of the train, and payments by credit card are accepted. you can book through the official e-ticketing website, or you may book an e-ticket with an agency (against THB 100 service fee).

A word of advice is to only listen to the people at the information desk anyone else walking around offering to help you "find" a hotel or taxi is just a tout, even if they are wearing official-looking badges. Likewise, the second floor shops offering "Tourist Information" are just agents in disguise. The taxi pick up and drop off point is to the left of the platforms as you walk towards them, and is generally chaotic at busy periods with scant regard for any queue. The left luggage facility is at the opposite end of the concourse, on the far right as you walk away from the platforms.

If coming by train from the north or north-east, connecting to the metro at Bang Sue Train Station can shave the last half-hour off your train trip. This is not a very good place to board trains though, as there is practically no information or signs in English. However, this situation will doubtlessly improve as more and more long-distance departures are switched to here from Hualamphong Train Station to ease congestion in the inner city.

The Thon Buri Train Station, formerly known as the Bangkok Noi Station, is on the west side of the river in Thonburi. It is the terminus for twice-daily trains to Kanchanaburi (via Nakhon Pathom). Just to keep things confusing, the previous Thonburi Train Station right next to the river (accessible by the Chao Phraya Express Boat pier Railway Station) is now mothballed and turned into a museum, but it's only 800m away from the new station. Note that the weekend-only second class air-conditioned "tourist" trains to Kanchanaburi and Nam Tok depart from Hualamphong Train Station.

Wongwien Yai Train Station only serves the rustic Mae Klong commuter line to the fishing village of Maha Chai. Trains run roughly hourly and the trip takes about one hour. The ride is of little interest if you want to get there fast, but is an experience for rail fans and an attraction in itself, with a nice view on the countryside's orchards, vegetable plantations and coconut groves. Maha Chai is a nice seafood destination, and if you feel like it, you can cross the Tha Chin river by ferry and continue by rail to Samut Songkhram. Wongwien Yai Train Station is about 800m from the Skytrain station of the same name; to get there, take a metered taxi for 35-50 baht, or walk (using a map). If you want to walk, continue in the same direction the train came from about 300 metres. You will see a main road underneath at right angles, so cross this and go to the right along this road. About another 300 metres along this road you will see an overhead walkway. Just beyond this on the left is a laneway to the on-ground station.

By ship

Not many people come to Bangkok by ship, but there are some cruise ships that come close to the city. Large ships must dock at Laem Chabang Port, about 90 minutes southeast of Bangkok and about 30 min north of Pattaya.

Frequent first and second class bus services directly connect Laem Chabang with Bangkok's Eastern Bus Terminal (Ekkamai); less frequent direct services run to the Northern Bus Terminal (Mo Chit). A first class air-conditioned bus (blue and white) to either will take 90min or less; the fare is around 100 baht. A quick way to get into downtown is to board an Ekkamai-bound bus and then disembark early at On Nut, where you can hop onto the Skytrain. The bus will always stop here if a passenger requests it.

Southbound buses en route to Pattaya can be boarded at the traffic lights on Sukhumvit Road in Laem Chabang. These are extremely frequent (at least 10 per hour), and charge less than 50 baht.

Modest-sized ships may dock further upriver at Khlong Toei Port, close to Bangkok's city centre. A modest terminal provides processing for passengers (who may receive Thai customs and immigration processing on-board), as well as offering "managers" who arrange tours and taxis. Reaching major hotels and other points of interest is much cheaper than from Laem Chabang, but can vary according to the passenger's negotiating skills. The facility is not close to the MRT stop of Khlong Toei, the best way to get there is by metered taxi.

By car
Getting into Bangkok by car is not a good idea, as you can easily waste half a day waiting in traffic just to get to the other side of the city. Three major highways lead to Bangkok from all directions of Thailand. The best way to get to Bangkok from Northern Thailand is driving on Phahonyothin Road(Route 1), which comes from Mae Sai near the Myanmarese border.

Sukhumvit Road (Route 3) comes from cities in Eastern Thailand, such as Trat, Pattaya and Chonburi.

Phetkasem Road (Route 4) must be one of the longest roads in the world, as it comes all the way from the Malaysian border serving Southern Thailand.

To ease congestion on these highways, a new system of motorways has emerged which will be extended in the future. The New Bangkok-Chonburi Motorway (Motorway 7) is covering the trip from Chonburi and Pattaya. Then there's the Kanchanaphisek National Highway (Motorway 9 or "Outer Ring Road") which makes a giant loop around Bangkok serving most satellite towns around it, such as Nonthaburi and Samut Prakan.

Getting around

The first phase of Bangkok's ambitious public transport system is now complete, the city's public transport system is fairly efficient and convenient, but there is still a fair amount of room for improvement to the system's integration.

The city, like many developing cities, suffers from paralytic traffic jams periodically throughout the day. In rush hours, it may be worthwhile combining public transport by different means. For example: soar over traffic jams by skytrain to the station closest to your destination and thereafter take a taxi for the final leg.

Bangkok is one of the most interesting cities in the world and is known to be number one for scenery. Perhaps you would like to know how to move around the city. There are many different ways to move around Bangkok. For example, using buses or Taxis, or maybe even on the water with a Ferry, or the public transit systems of BTS and MRT.

By public transit
Skytrain

The BTS Skytrain (รถไฟฟ้าบีทีเอส *rot fai fa BTS*, pronounced *bee-tee-et*) deserves a visit simply for the Disneyland space-ageness of it. Built in a desperate effort to ease Bangkok's insane traffic and pollution, the Skytrain covers most of downtown and is especially convenient for visiting Siam Square. There are two lines: the light green Sukhumvit Line travels along Sukhumvit Road, Siam Square and then follows Phahonyothin Road up north, where it terminates at Mo Chit (N8), near the Chatuchak Weekend Market. The dark green Silom Line starts in Thonburi, passes the Express Boat pier at Saphan Taksin (S6), goes through the Silom area and ends at National Stadium (W1), right next to MBK Center. Both lines come together at Siam(CEN), where you can interchange between them. Unfortunately, there is no station near Khao San Road, but you can take the Express Boat from Phra Arthit Pier to Sathorn Pier, where you can switch onto the Skytrain.

You must have 5 or 10 baht coins to purchase Skytrain tickets from vending machines, so hold on to them. At most stations there is a single touchscreen machine that will accept 20, 50 and 100 baht notes, but there is often a queue to use it. Some stations have ticket counters which will change your large bills so you can purchase tickets from the vending machines. Fares range from 15 to 52 baht depending upon how many zones you are travelling. Consult the map (in English) near each ticket machine. If you do not have coins, queue for change from the staff at the booth. If you are in town for several days (or going to make several visits during the next 30 days), weigh your options and consider a rechargeable stored-value card (from 100 baht, with a 30 baht refundable deposit and a 30 baht non-refundable card cost), a "ride all you like" **tourist** pass (140 baht per day) or a multiple ride pass of 20 trips or more to any zone (15 trips cost 345 baht, 25 trips cost 550 baht; plus a 30 baht refundable deposit for a rechargeable card that is valid for 5 years). They will certainly save you time, scrambling for coins, and maybe even money. Check for information with the English speaking staff.

In 2013 the Silom Line was extended westward from Talat Phul (S10) to Bang Wa (S12).

Metro
The MRT (รถไฟฟ้ามหานคร *rot fai tai din*, pronounced *em-ar-tee*) finally opened in July 2004. There are two lines, the Blue Line and the new Purple Line . The Blue Line connects the central Hualamphong Train Station (1) to the northern Bang Sue Train Station (18), running through Silom, Sukhumvit, Ratchadaphisek and area around Chatuchak Weekend Market in Phahonyothin. There are interchanges to the Skytrain at Si Lom (3), Sukhumvit (7) and Chatuchak Park (16) stations. The section from Bang Sue to Tao Poon where it connects with the new Purple Line, which runs northwestward, serving suburban area and Nonthaburi Province nearby.

Tourists do not use the metro as much as the Skytrain, but there are some useful stops. The terminus at Hua Lamphong (1) provides a good access to Yaowarat. If you're going to the Chatuchak Weekend Market, don't get out at Chatuchak Park, but go one stop further to Kamphaeng Phet (17) as it drops you right inside the market.

Metro tickets are not interchangeable with Skytrain tickets. Rides start from 16 baht and are based on distance; pre-paid cards of up to 1,000 baht are also available. For single ride fares, a round plastic token is used. It is electronic: simply wave it by the scanner to enter; deposit it in a slot by the exit gate leave.

Bag-checks take place at the entrance to each station. It's usually nothing more than a quick peek inside, unless you are looking particularly suspicious.

Airport Rail Link

Finally opened in August 2010 is the Airport Rail Link (รถไฟฟ้าเชื่อมท่าอากาศยานสุวรรณภูมิ). Many Thais in Eastern Bangkok use the link to commute to the city centre. It starts at Suvarnabhumi Airport and terminates at Phaya Thai, with some interesting stops in between (such as Ramkhamhaeng and Ratchaprarop for Pratunam). A ride costs 15-45 baht, depending on distance. Trains run every 15min 06:00-23:59.

From Makkasan, you can continue your way by metro at Phetchaburi MRT station. The transfer can be made via the pedestrian bridge which was opened in June 2013. From Phaya Thai, you can transfer onto the Skytrain, but be aware that there are not enough lifts yet, and those available are too small for large pieces of luggage. New lifts will be installed in Ramkhamhaeng, Ratchaprarop and Phaya Thai stations in the following months.

BRT Sathon-Ratchaphruek Line

The 16km (9.9 mi) route has twelve stations in the centre of the road that give level access to the right hand side of the buses. The first route from Sathon to Ratchaphruek via Narathiwat Ratchanakharin and Rama III roads, opened to the public in 2010 and both terminuses connect to the Silom Line of the BTS Skytrain; at Chong Nonsi (S3) and at Talat Phlu (S10).

SRT Light Red Line

The Light Red Line (รถไฟฟ้าชานเมืองสายสีแดงอ่อน) is part of the planned Red Line suburban railway system to serve the Bangkok Metropolitan Region. The segment from Taling Chan to Bang Son (15 km) opened for limited, free trial service in Dec 2012. Only 6 services a day currently operate on this line. This train system currently does not connect with any of the other train lines in Bangkok. The final section to Bang Sue station of this first phase will not open until the new Bang Sue Terminal is constructed.

By boat

Chao Phraya River should be high on any tourist's agenda. The cheapest and most popular option is the Chao Phraya Express Boat, basically an aquatic bus plying up and down the river. The basic service plies from Wat Rajsingkorn (S4) all the way north to Nonthaburi (N30), with stops at most of Rattanakosin's major attractions including the Grand Palace (at Tha Chang) and Wat Pho (at Tha Tien). The closest pier to Khao San Road is Phra Arthit. Enter the express boat at the numerous piers and pay for the trip at ticket collector, who will approach you bearing a long metal cylinder. At some bigger piers you can buy the ticket before boarding. When the metal cylinder lady approaches you, just show her the ticket you bought on the pier.

The different boat lines are indicated by the colours of the flags at the top of the boat. These flags can be confusing; don't think the yellow King's flag corresponds to the yellow line flag! There is a basic "no flag" line (9, 11 or 13 baht) that goes along all the piers, but it only runs during rush hours (M-F 06:20-8:05 and 15:00-17:30) and is fairly slow. It's better to take the faster yellow (19 or 28 baht, M-F 06:15-08:10 and 15:30-18:05) and orange (15 baht, daily 06:00-19:00) flag lines, but you have to be sure where you're going as they don't stop everywhere. The yellow line is the fastest, but is best avoided as it skips many popular attractions (including Khao San Road, the Grand Palace and Wat Pho). The orange line is your best bet, as it covers the major tourist areas and is fairly quick too.

In addition to the workaday express boat, there is also a blue flagged Tourist Boat which stops at a different subset of piers, offers commentary in English and charges 150 baht for a day pass. Single tickets are 50 baht. The boats are slightly more comfortable and may be worth considering if you want to cruise up and down the most important tourist sights. They only operate once per 30 minutes and stop running by 15:00. Be careful as they may tell you the (cheaper) orange flag regular boat is not coming for quite a while (as they are aggressively touting for business), but sometimes this is not the truth. If you want the tourist experience with guide and (very) loud speaker commentary, often unintelligible, then this is the one for you. However, be aware that you are fully entitled to enter the public piers (the ones with the blue lettering on white background with pier numbers on them) and get the orange flag boat as these are public places and you don't need a ticket before boarding the comfortable and speedy orange-flag boat.

The signposting of the piers is quite clear, with numbered piers and English route maps. Sathorn (Taksin) pier has been dubbed "Central" station, as it offers an quick interchange to Saphan Taksin BTS station. The boats run every 5-20 minutes from sunrise to sunset (roughly 06:00-19:00), so ignore any river taxi touts who try to convince you otherwise.

Many piers are also served by cross-river ferries. These are particularly useful for reaching Wat Arun or the many piers at the Thonburi side of the river. Cross-river ferries run around every 10 minutes and only cost 5 baht pay at the kiosk on the pier and then walk through the turnstile.

Express Boat serves the long Saen Saep Canal, one of the remaining canals (*khlong*) that used to flow through Bangkok. Mostly used by locals to commute to work, the service is cheap and you get to see the 'backside' of the neighbourhoods, so to speak. Also, It is immune to Bangkok's notorious traffic jams. The total distance is 18 km, and the service operates from 05:30-20:30.

They are comparatively safe just watch your step when boarding and disembarking as they don't stop at the pier for long and do not let the dirty water get into your eyes. To prevent splashes, the boats are equipped with little curtains that you can raise by pulling on a string, but they have to be lowered at every stop so people can clamber on board. It's better to sit closer to the front of the boat further away from the engine which can be quite loud. Pay the fare (10-20 baht) to the fearless helmet-wearing ticket collectors who clamber around on the outside of the boat, ducking at bridges, as it barrels down the canal. Press the green 'bell' button if you want to get off at the next pier, else the boat might just skip it. The piers now even have (tiny) signs in English.

The canal runs parallel to Phetchaburi Road, and provides the easiest access from the Golden Mount in Rattanakosin (and nearby Khao San Road) to Siam Square and Pratunam. This line is aptly called the Golden Mount Line and runs from Panfa Leelard pier to Pratunam pier in downtown. If you want to continue your journey beyond Pratunam, passengers have to change boats there. The NIDA Line starts at Pratunam and heads east to Sukhumvit and Ramkhamhaeng. Hold on to your ticket.

River taxi

Finally, for trips outside set routes, you can hire a long-tail river taxi at any major pier. These are fairly expensive and will attempt to charge as much as 1,000 baht/h for foreigners, but with some haggling they may be suitable for small groups. To circumvent the Mafia-like touts who attempt to get a large cut for every ride, agree for the price of the shortest possible ride (30min), then negotiate directly with the captain when on board.

By taxi

Metered taxi

Metered taxis are a quick and comfortable way to get around town, at least if the traffic is flowing your way, but be warned that Bangkok taxi drivers are notorious for finding ways to run up the fare for foreigners; insist that the meter is used, and if the driver claims that your destination is closed, that he doesn't know where it is, or if he tries to take you elsewhere, just get out of the taxi. All taxis are now metered and air-conditioned: the hailing fee is 35 baht and most trips within the city centre cost less than 100 baht. There are no surcharges (except from the airport), even at night; don't believe drivers who try to tell you otherwise. A red sign on the front window, if lit, means that the taxi is available.

When the meter is switched on you will see a red '35' somewhere on the dashboard or between the driver and you. Be sure to check for this at the start of the ride, as many drivers will "forget" to start the meter in order to overcharge you at the end of your trip. Most will start the meter when asked politely to do so (*meter na khrap* if you're male and *meter na kha* if you're female); if the driver refuses to use the meter after a couple of attempts, simply exit the taxi.

In some cases, late at night and especially near major tourist districts like Khao San or Patpong, you will need to walk a block away to catch a honest driver. The effort can save you as much as 150 baht. This is often also the case for taxis that park all day in front of your hotel. There are only two reasons that they are there: to take you places where they can get their commissions (jewellery stores, tailors, massage parlours, etc.) and to overcharge you by not using the meter.

Your best bet is to walk to the road and catch an unoccupied metered taxi in motion (easier than it sounds, as Bangkok traffic tends to crawl the majority of the time, and one car out of four is a taxi). Avoid parked taxis altogether, and if a taxi driver refuses to turn the meter on, simply close the door and find one who will. Keep in mind that it is illegal for them to have un-metered fares. Be smart and give your money to honest drivers, not touts. The only reason that they get away with this so frequently is that foreign tourists let them.

Be sure to either know the correct pronunciation of your destination, or have it written in Thai, as taxi drivers in Bangkok are notoriously bad at reading maps, and most drivers speak limited English. Most hotels and guest houses will happily write out addresses in Thai for you. While most drivers will recognise the names of tourist hot spots, even if grossly mispronounced, but it is often difficult to properly pronounce addresses in Thai. If your mobile phone works in Thailand, it is sometimes useful to call your hotel and ask the staff to speak to your driver in Thai. In addition, try to get your hotel's business card to show the taxi driver in case you get lost.

If you are pinching pennies or fussy about your means of transportation, you may wish to avoid getting into one of the (very common) yellow-green taxis. They are owner-operated and of highly variable quality and occasionally have rigged meters. All other colours belong to large taxi companies, which usually enforce their standards better.

On some routes, the driver will ask if he should use the *tollway* this will usually save a lot of time. You have to pay the cost at the toll booth (not in advance and not at the end of the journey). Watch how much the driver really pays, as many try to keep the change.

When getting out, try to have small bills (100 baht or less) or expect problems with change. Tips are not necessary, but are certainly welcome if you're happy about the service; most local passengers will round up or leave any coin change as tip.

Grab, Uber, and other apps

These modern apps make "taxi" rides more straightforward, less prone to scams, and often a bit cheaper than ordinary taxis. There's no need to attempt to pronounce the destination in Thai because you simply type it in the app. Drivers expect a cash payment, so you don't need to enter your credit card in the app.

When you have a confirmed driver on Grab or Uber, check the car model and plate number in the app. Then wait for the car to get near you (shown on the map) and wave your hand when you see the car.

Standard cars are usually relatively new Toyota Vios, Honda City, or similar very small 4-door sedans. They are comfortable for 3 passengers and one suit case in the trunk, but it's better to opt for a minivan if any more room is needed.

Tuk-tuk

Finally, what would Bangkok be without the much-loathed, much-loved tuk-tuks? You'll know them when you hear them, and you'll hate them when you smell them these three-wheeled contraptions blaze around Bangkok leaving a black cloud of smog in their wake. For anything more than a 5-10 min jaunt or just the experience, they really are not worth the price but it can still be enjoyable for people that come to Thailand and, if you let them get away with it, the price will usually be 4 or 5 times what it should be anyway (which, for Thais, is around 30% less than the equivalent metered taxi fare).

On the other hand, you can sometimes ride for free if you agree to visit touristy clothing or jewellery shops (which give the tuk-tuk driver fuel coupons and commissions for bringing customers). The shops' salesmen are pushy, and try to scam you with bad quality suits or "gems" that in fact are worthless pieces of cut glass. But usually you are free to leave after 5-10min of browsing. Visitors should beware though, sometimes one stop can turn in to three, and your tuk-tuk driver may not be interested in taking you where you need to go once he has his fuel coupons. Also, with Bangkok's densely congested traffic it is sure to waste hours of your time, if not the whole day.

If you still want to try the tuk-tuk, always hail a moving tuk-tuk from the main road. At tourist spots, these tuk-tuk drivers lie in waiting to disrupt your travels plans. Always agree on a price before entering the tuk-tuk. Also be crystal clear about your intended destination. If they claim that your intended destination is closed for the day, and offer to take you to other nearby tourist spots, insist on your destination or get out. If you're an all-male party, tuk-tuk drivers sometimes will just ignore your destination completely and start driving you to some brothel ("beautiful girls"). Insist continually and forcefully on going only to your destination; or take a metered taxi instead. Or alternatively, there is a hop on hop off tuk-tuk service that allows you to hop around Bangkok attractions.

A songthaew is a converted pick-up truck that usually serves the back sois in residential neighbourhoods. They usually have four wheels instead of three, two benches instead of one, run on petrol instead of LPG and resemble a tiny truck. The maids and locals tend to use them to return home from the market with loads of groceries, or for quick trips if they're available. The fare is seven baht, which is paid to the driver when you get out. Neither the fare nor the route is negotiable. Just wave one down and hop in then ring the bell when you want to get out and hand the driver 7 baht. No English is spoken and there's no need to speak to the driver anyway.

Motorbike taxi

When traffic slows to a crawl and there are no mass-transit alternatives for your destination, by far the fastest mode of transport is a motorbike taxi (มอเตอร์ไซค์รับจ้าง *motosai lapjang*). The people in the coloured tabards are motosai cabbies. They typically wear colourful fluorescent yellow-orange or red vests and wait for passengers at busy places. Prices are negotiable before you ride but is the best way when the traffic is not flowing as well as usual in Bangkok (!).

For the adrenaline junkie, a wild motosai ride can provide a fantastic rush. Imagine weaving through rows of stopped vehicles at 50 km/h (30 mph) with mere centimetres to spare on each side, dodging pedestrians, other motorbikes, tuk-tuks, stray dogs and the occasional elephant while the driver blithely ignores all traffic laws and even some laws of physics. Now do the same while facing backwards on the bike and balancing a large television on your lap, and then you can qualify as a local though you might die in the process. Imagine your loved ones arranging to ship your dead body home from Bangkok because you took a dangerous risk you were warned not to. Motorcycle accidents are brutally common, and transportation of this sort is inherently hazardous. Be aware of the risk before using motorcycle taxis. Many tourists and Thai alike recommend avoiding them except as a last resort. Under no circumstances ride without a helmet.

The overwhelming majority of motorcycle taxis do not travel long distances, but simply shuttle up and down long sois (side-streets) not serviced by other transport for a fixed 5-20 baht fare. These are marginally less dangerous, especially if you happen to travel with the flow on a one-way street.

The law requires that both driver and passenger must wear a helmet. It is the driver's responsibility to provide you with one, so if you are stopped by police, any fine is also the driver's responsibility. This is worth bearing in mind when you hire a motorbike or moped. Make sure that if there are two of you, the hirer provides two helmets instead of one. When riding, keep a firm grasp on the seat handle and watch out for your knees.

By bus

Local buses, operated by the Bangkok Mass Transit Authority (องค์การขนส่งมวลชนกรุงเทพ) or just BMTA (ขสมก), are the cheapest but also the most challenging way of getting around. There is a bewildering plethora of routes, usually marked only in Thai. Even Thais have a hard time with these, but at least they can call the 1384 Bus Route Hotline, which is in Thai only. However you can also use Google's transit planner function on Google Maps to plan your bus journeys. Please note, however, that the bus arrival times on Google Maps may not actually correlate to the actual bus arrival time. Bus stops list only the bus numbers that stop there and nothing more. They are also subject to Bangkok's notorious traffic, often terribly crowded, and many are not air-conditioned. If you want to get somewhere quickly and are not prepared to get lost, the buses should be avoided (remember that taxis are cheaper than most local buses in the West). However, they make for a good adventure if you're not in a rush and you don't mind being the centre of attention by loving Thais. In Victory Momunent where many buses go to there are some uniformed people that seem to know the whole bus system in Bangkok. Try to find them, they are very helpful and work perfectly.

But for the intrepid, and those staying in Khao San Road where buses are the only practical means of public transport, the official resource for decrypting bus routes is the BMTA website. It has up-to-date if slightly incomplete listings of bus routes in English, but no maps. Another site in English which also features a route planner is Transit Bangkok. You can also ask your guest house about which buses to take if you're going to a particular destination. As a printed reference, the 69 baht spent on the *Bangkok Bus Map* by Roadway is a good investment if you're going to travel by bus more than once.

The hierarchy of Bangkok's buses from cheapest to best can be ranked as follows:

> **Small orange bus**, 8 baht flat fare. Cramped, no air-con, no fan, famously suicidal drivers, usually not advisable for more than short hops. Run by private operators, they can be significantly faster than the BMTA-run buses.

> **Red bus**, 6.50 baht fare. More spacious and fan-cooled (in theory). Unlike other buses, some of these operate through the night (1.50 baht surcharge). These buses are BMTA-run.

➢ **White/blue bus**, 8 baht fare. Exactly the same as the red buses, but cost one baht more. These buses are owned by private entities operated in conjunction with BMTA.

➢ **Blue/yellow and cream/blue air-con**, 10 baht for the first 8km (5 mi), up to 18 baht max. These buses are quite comfy. The blue/yellow striped buses are privately owned while the blue/cream buses are BMTA-owned.

➢ **Orange air-con (Euro II)**, 11 baht for the first few kilometres, up to 23 baht maximum. These are all BMTA-run, newer, and more comfortable.

➢ **Pink/white micro-buses**, 20 baht flat fare, paid into a fare-collection machine located next to the driver exact fare only. Not quite common away from the city centre, these are air-conditioned, modern and only allow seated passengers (making them harder to use at rush hour as many won't stop for you).

Some useful bus lines to any well-known places inaccessible by either BTS or MRT are as follows (click on the numbers for the maps):

➢ 15: This route provides the connection between Khao San Road and the BTS stations around Siam Square & Silom.

➢ 47: This route is similar to Line 15 and acts as a supplementary service.

> 53: This circular route travels through the older areas of Bangkok, including Ko Rattanakosin and the Chinatown. One may continue by MRT Hualamphong for Bangkok Train Station & shopping centres.

> 59: This route is useful for those who want to get into the city centre from Don Mueang Airport to the BTS or Khao San Road.

> 79: This route is very important to travelers due to it passing many touristy places. Destinations include:

>> BTS Siam

>> Shopping areas (Siam Square, Ratchaprasong, Pratunam)

>> Khao San Road, Sanam Luang & Grand Palace (walking)

>> Taling Chan Floating Market

>> Southern Bus Terminal

> 509: Tourists can use this bus line to travel from Khao San Road to the Northern Bus Terminal, as well as the Dusit area.

> 515: 515 provides the quick access to the Southern Bus Terminal from the city centre. Also, it passes near the Dusit area.

> ➢ 554: DMK <-> BKK airport link

Buses stop only when needed, so wave them down (arm out, palm down) when you see one barrelling your way. Pay the roaming collector after you board and keep the ticket, as there can be occasional spot-checks. Press the signal buzzer (usually near the door) when you want to get off.

Two further pitfalls are that buses of the same number may run slightly different routes depending on the colour, and there are also express services (mostly indicated by yellow signs) that skip some stops and may take the expressway (2 baht extra).

Airport buses allow luggage (backpacks and suitcases), but regular buses do not. Enforcement of this rule varies

By Car
Bangkok has good quality roads, but driving in the city can be a nightmare with massive traffic jams, a convoluted web of expressways and oft-confusing road signs. If driving, be especially aware of sudden lane changes by cars and reckless motorcyclists who tend to weave in and out of traffic. On busy roads you will often find vehicles moving slowly into the traffic from car parks and side streets, those already on the road are expected to give way.

Do not park on the road in busy districts such as Siam because other cars might lock you in by parking next to you in the 2nd or 3rd lane.

Use covered car parks or park a bit off the beaten path, and then walk back. If using a car park and there are no marked bays available, you can park in front of other cars, but make sure you leave the car in neutral with the parking brake off so you can be rolled out of the way if required. Similarly, if you've parked in a marked bay and are blocked by another car, simply push it out of the way - carefully.

Renting a car is an option for travelling in Bangkok and other parts of Thailand. Always get the optional insurance - the basic rental charge usually doesn't have any insurance at all, and your travel insurance is only likely to cover an excess or deductible where there is some basic level of insurance. Check the policy carefully for exclusions, at least some policies exclude speeding and advise that this is monitored by GPS.

Seeing

Most of Bangkok's sights are concentrated on the island of Rattanakosin, often referred to as the "Old City". Out of Bangkok's hundreds of temples, the Grand Palace, Wat Pho and Wat Arun usually make up the top 3. The Grand Palace has an immense size, so expect to spend at least a full morning or afternoon there. Within the palace grounds is Wat Phra Kaew, the most sacred Buddhist temple of Thailand. Unlike other temples, it is not one building, nor are there living spaces for monks. Instead, it is a collection of highly decorated holy buildings and monuments. One of its buildings houses the Emerald Buddha, and while you might not expect it from its size, it is the most sacred Buddha image of Thailand. Sadly the entrance fee is quite steep (500 Bhat, August 2016) for what you get. There are basically only two buildings you can enter and the whole area is absolutely overcrowded. Huge loads of tourists everywhere, it feels like a zoo or Disneyland. It kind of ruins the experience.

Nearby is Wat Pho, home to the world's largest reclining Buddha image and a famed massage school. Entrance Fee is 100 Bhat and you get a free water + you can refill your water bottles inside. Regarding to the ticket its open to 6:30 pm. (August 2016). Take the ferry across the Chao Phraya River to Thonburi for the outstanding Wat Arun. The main structure is about 60-88 m high and it is surrounded by four smaller prangs. It is one of Thailand's most picturesque temples, and is engraved on the inner part of all ten-baht coins. It is so recognisable that it even became the logo of the Tourism Authority of Thailand (TAT). If you look closely, you will see that it is beautifully decorated with colourful broken Chinese porcelain pieces. It is currently being renovated and the majority is covered in scaffolding. Climbing up is also prohibited due to the renovations. Heading back to Rattanakosin, there are many other major temples you could visit, including the Golden Mount, Wat Suthat and Wat Ratchanaddaram.

Don't throw away the entry ticket of the Grand Palace, as it gives free entry to the Dusit Palace in Dusit. It is situated in a leafy, European-style area built by King Rama V to escape the heat of the Grand Palace. Its main structure is the Vimanmek Mansion, touted as the largest golden teakwood house in the world, but you could spend your whole day in the museums if you wish. There are many museums in Bangkok showing traditional Thai-style residences. Most visitors take a tour through Jim Thompson's House, the CIA-operative's mansion assembled by combining six traditional Thai-style houses, conveniently located near Siam Square.

Ban Kamthieng in Sukhumvit, M.R. Kukrit's Heritage Home in Silom and the Suan Pakkad Palace in Phahonyothin are not quite as impressive, but still make for a nice experience. Rattanakosin's museums are mostly dedicated to history and culture, including the National Museum (about Thai history and archaeological remains), the Museum of Siam and the King Prajadhipok Museum. Bangkok has a small, but vocal art community, and you might want to visit the National Gallery or The Queen's Gallery, or one of its numerous smaller galleries spread over the city. Siam Square features the recently opened Bangkok Art and Culture Centre which has temporary art exhibitions throughout year.

Lumphini Park in Silom is the largest park in central Bangkok, and a good way to escape the fumes. Backpackers around Khao San Road can head for Santichaiprakarn Park, a small but fun park along the Chao Phraya River with a breezy atmosphere, usually with locals juggling or practicing tricks. It is built around the 18th-century Phra Sumen Fortwith a nice view on the modern Rama VIII cable-stayed bridge. Zoos and animal farms are some of the more popular tourist attractions in Bangkok, but before visiting, please be aware that animal welfare in Thailand is not strictly regulated. Poor living conditions of the animals and inadequate veterinary care are examples of the sad mistreatment of the animal population. You can't go wrong at the Queen Saovabha Institute Snake Farm in Silom, as the staff takes good care of their snakes and they have a job of informing the public about the risks associated with them. Another nice family attraction is Siam Ocean World in Siam Square. It has a steep price tag, but at least you get to see the largest aquarium in Southeast Asia.

PAK NAM temple is located on Petch Kasem road. This place is quite peaceful because less people go there. Beside the temple, there is a big canal located for you to feed the fishes. And the Architecture here is also very nice and so amazing that the wall of this temple is neatly carved to describe about the history of the Buddhism and most of the parts of this temple are made up of teak woods.

Doing
Tuk Tuk tours

The Tuk Tuk is one of the symbols of Bangkok so there is no better way to explore Bangkok than by whizzing around the streets in one of these iconic three wheeled vehicles. You can pick up a tuk tuk on any street corner (and the price you will be charged could vary hugely) but there are also many tour operators who also run tours which use a tuk tuk as the main form of transport.

There is also a Tuk Tuk hop on hop off service that travelers can pay once and hop around top Bangkok attractions around Rattanakosin, Khao San Road, Dusit, Yaowarat and Phahurat areas.

Bicycle tours

Cycling in Bangkok may sound crazy, as cycling is deadly dangerous on the main roads, but it certainly is not if you know where to go. Away from the main roads there is a vast system of small streets and alleys. Cyclists are treated as pedestrians, so you can use your bicycle to explore parks, temple complexes, markets and the more quiet residential areas of eastern Bangkok. In more crowded places you can cycle on the pavement. Exploring the town by bicycle has all the advantages of going by foot, combined with a much greater action radius and a cooling breeze.

If you want to experience Bangkok hideaways and countryside, leisurely cycling through green paddy fields, colourful orchid farms, peaceful lotus fields and touched by the charm of Thai way of country life at personal level, bicycle is a great way to do it. There are a handful of specialist operators that offer daily or regular departures to the so-called "Bangkok jungle" (Bang Kachao), a semi-island across the river from Bangkok with few cars or buildings, or through the backstreets of Chinatown. It sounds strange but a cycle tour in Bangkok really is the best way to discover the city up close.

Project Bangkok Smile Bike subsidized by city allowes free bike rental even without deposit just with photo of your passport.

> ➤ **Co van Kessel**,+66 2 639-7351. Co van Kessel offers many cycling tours through Bangkok, taking in Chinatown, the canals of Thonburi, the "Bangkok Jungle" and many other places in between. 950-1,950 baht.

> ➤ **Follow Me Bicycle Tours**, 126 Sathorn Tai Rd, +66 2 286-5891. Follow Me offers half-day bicycle tours through Bangkok's residential streets. Included in the asking price is a fish spa and a barbecue meal after the tour. 1,000 baht.

> ➤ **'Go' Bangkok Bicycle Tours**, 69/2-3-4 Charoen Krung Soi 44, +66 2 103 4731 , fax: 66 02 103 4731),. 9am-10pm. Go Bangkok Tours offers half & full day bicycle tours (Guided-Self Guided through Bangkok's residential streets. Included in the asking price are helmets and insurance. 600 baht.

> ➤ **Grasshopper Adventures**, 57 Ratchadamnoen Klang Rd (*near the Democracy Monument, right around the corner from Khao*

San Rd), +66 2 280-0832, Grasshopper Adventures operates tours through the historic Rattanakosin district of Bangkok, to the outskirts of Bangkok and one that takes place at night. Tours regularly book out so make a reservation in advance. 1,000-1,600 baht.

➢ **Recreational Bangkok Biking** (*RBB*), Baan Sri Kung 350/127, Soi 71, Rama III Road, Yannawa, +66 2-285 3955. Recreational Bangkok Biking, operates daily bicycle tours in small groups only (a maximum of 8 participants). Colours of Bangkok starts every day, 08:00 & 13:00. Book in advance as availability is limited. THB 1,000.

➢ **SpiceRoads**, +66 2 712-5303. 1,000-2,500 baht. They offer many 1 day and multi-day cycling trips in and around Bangkok. There are trips to the Bangkok Jungle, Ko Kret, Yaowarat, and Thonburi.

➢ **Thailand Green Ride** +66 2 888-9637. These are "green rides", half-day, 1 day and home stay overnight cycling trips through the green countryside of Bangkok.

Bangkok On the Run

Cycling is a popular option among tour companies, but there are a variety of running clubs in Bangkok that welcome visitors multiple times per week for running, socializing, eating and drinking throughout Bangkok and the surrounding areas. These clubs are either free or charge a small, non-profit fee to pay for food and drink served at the event.

Running is a great way to see parts of the city and countryside that you'd never otherwise experience. If you go with a social running club, it's also a great chance to meet interesting people, eat food you've never tried and to make new friends. If you're interested in seeing countryside, out-of-the-way districts, plantations, jungle and other places you can only go on foot, you might be interested in these clubs:

➢ **The Bangkok Hash,**. The Bangkok Hash is the original hash in Bangkok, started in 1977 and running every Saturday (check web site for directions and times). It's a traditional men-only hash that welcomes male visitors of all ages of the running and walking variety who want to run in interesting areas, drink a little beer and socialize over Thai food afterwards. 300 Baht Run Fee (Visitors).

➢ **The Bangkok Monday Hash**. The Bangkok Monday Hash, founded in 1982, runs every Monday later afternoon around 17:00 depending on the time of year (check web site for directions and times). It's a co-ed hash that welcomes all visitors, both runners and walkers, of all ages for a good run, some cold beer and an optional meal afterwards. 250 Baht Run Fee.

➤ **Siam Sunday Hash House Harriers**. The Siam Sunday Hash House Harriers were founded in 1997 as a co-ed, laid back hash that welcomes all visitors (runners and walkers). The hash runs on the first and third Sunday of every month around 16:30 depending on the time of year (check web site for directions and times) and visitors can reliably meet at the Rama VI statue in front of Lumpini Park to catch a ride. Like all other traditional Bangkok hashes, you're welcome for a good run or walk, some cold beer and an optional meal afterwards. 250 baht Run Fee (Male Visitors) / 150 baht Run Fee (Female Visitors).

➤ **The Bangkok Harriettes**. The Bangkok Harriettes, devised as a female hash, were founded in 1982 welcomes visitors both male and female. The hash runs every Wednesday 17:00 depending on the time of year (check web site for directions and times). Beer is included in the run fee and you're welcome to move on to an adjacent restaurant afterwards. 250 baht Run Fee (Male Visitors) / 150 baht Run Fee (Female Visitors).

➤ **Run My City: Bangkok**. Run My City is an upstart event for visitors (or locals) who just want to come out and run parts of the city that are otherwise unseen. There's no fee and no real rules as the host of each Run My City event sets their own agenda for the group. Run My City: Bangkok runs at least once a month, more based on attendance, with events posted on their

Facebook Page. Anyone who can run at least 5-10 km in an hour is welcome to this low-pressure, non-racing running event. Free.

Nature tours

Flight of the Gibbon, +66 53 010660 . Zipline through the lush rainforest, just outside of Bangkok. 3 km of ziplines connect to 24 platform stations, lookout platforms, lowering stations, and sky bridges, making the experience a full zipline canopy tour. The tour also includes a free tram tour around Khao Kheow Open Safari Park.

Canal tours

Another great way to see the Chao Phraya River and the original canals of the city is by canal tour. Most of these special boat trips start at the eastern bank of the Chao Phraya and head through the backwaters of Thonburi, taking in Wat Arun, the Royal Barges National Museum and a floating market. More information about these canal tours can be found in the Thonburi article. At 1,000 baht or more, they are quite expensive though; a cheaper and also fun activity is to take the public express boat along the Chao Phraya River. You can get off anywhere between Thewet and Sathon (Taksin) piers as there are many things to see in all those neighbourhoods. You can even go all the way north to Nonthaburi in the morning, enjoy the afternoon in this laid-back traditional urban town and take the boat back around rush hour.

Muay Thai

Muay Thai, informally known as Thai Boxing, is both a sport and a means of self-defence. Contestants are allowed to use almost any part of the body: feet, elbows, legs, knees, and shoulders. There are two venues in Bangkok to see this type of sport in action, Lumpinee Boxing Stadium in Silom and Ratchadamnoen Stadium in Rattanakosin. Sessions can take the whole evening, and the more interesting fights tend to happen in the end, so it's not that bad if you come slightly too late. The playing of traditional music during the bouts is enjoyable as well. A downer is the steep 1,000-2,000 baht entry fee for foreigners, while Thais chip in for 100 baht or less.

Muay Thai venue outside MBK Center every Wednesday (starts at 18:00, lasts until around 21:00), and it's free.

There is also a local TV station (Channel 7), which has their own little fighting arena near Mo Chit BTR station. It is located on soi Ruamsirimitr street. But just ask people for boxing and Channel (Chang) 7. They will be able to show you the way. Fighting is every sunday. Entry is free, and this particular boxing will be shown and watched in TV all around Bangkok. Also with little knowledge of Thaiboxing you will be fascinated by the locals betting and cheering for their favorite.

Cultural performances

There are many cultural performances in Bangkok that shows traditional Thai culture and dance. Siam Niramit in Ratchadaphisek is a truly spectacular performance where more than 150 performers depict the history of each region of Thailand.

Of a completely different order are Bangkok's famous drag shows. These cabarets generally take about two hours, and besides singing, dancing, glamour and costumes, usually it also has some comedy thrown in. The most famous show is Calypso Cabaret in Ratchathewi that has two sessions every evening at the Asia Hotel. Always book these shows a couple of days in advance.

Pampering

Bangkok, a city of astonishing contrasts, is a truly amazing city by any standard. The ancient blends with the modern and somehow the combination works in surprising and interesting ways. Likewise with your personal lifestyle, you can choose to get a massage or learn Thai Massage at a beautiful Buddhist temple, or you may prefer the modern alternative: an urban health oasis where you are pampered and treated with your choice of therapies or techniques.

The respected Travel & Leisure Magazine Survey ranked Bangkok the world's #1 city in 2008 and 2010, and after spending some time there, you'll begin to understand why. The city has so much to offer, the prices are very reasonable, the attractions plentiful and diverse, the shopping superb, and the healthcare simply outstanding. It's not difficult to find the perfect place to take good care of you, be it a first-rate hospital, a modern dental clinic, or a beautiful spa or wellness centre

1. S Medical Spa - Winner of the AsiaSpa Awards 2007 Medi-Spa of the Year and one of Asia's leading medical spas; frequently ranked as one of the world's top ten spas.

2. TRIA Integrative Wellness Center, Piyavate Hospital - Winner of such awards as the SpaAsia Crystal Awards and AsiaSpa Awards 2008 another of Thailand's best and highly-rated spas.

3. The Oriental Spa, Mandarin Oriental Hotel like the hotel itself, in an exceptional class all its own.

Bangkok has scores of wonderful, popular, professional spas; some of the leading ones are Leyana Spa, Divana Spa, Mandara Spa, Spa de Bangkok, Devarana Spa Dusit Thani Hotel, The Oasis Spa Bangkok, Banyan Tree Spa Bangkok, and the Spa Cenvaree - Centara Grand at Central World.

Spas, traditionally, were towns where public baths, hospitals or hotels were built on top of mineral springs so that people could come and make use of the healing properties found in the water and its mud for medical purposes. These days, a spa doesn't have to be a town built on natural thermal springs. It can be a place anywhere that anyone can go to, to relax in tranquil surroundings with a variety of treatment administered to re-contour and rejuvenate the body and mind.

All self-respecting luxury hotels in Bangkok have a spa that at least offers a traditional Thai massage. Prices are exorbitant, but they offer some of the best treatments in Bangkok. Particularly well-regarded spas at exceptionally high rates are given at the splurge hotels in Silom. Independent spas offer much the same experience, but offer much more competitive rates. Figure around 2,000 baht/h for most treatments at the hotel spas and around 1,000 baht/h at the independent spas. However, it is worth researching before booking as prices can vary widely between establishments, and various promotions are often available. The best regarded hotel spas are at Mandarin Oriental, Plaza Athenee and The Eugenia. The best regarded independent spas are Oasis Spa, So Thai Spa and Divana Massage & Spa.

The ubiquitous little massage shops found on every street corner in town offer the best value for money, but the smallest range of services, with offerings usually limited to massage only. Particularly Khao San Road and Sukhumvit have plenty of these popular places. It is fairly easy to distinguish legitimate massage shops from more dubious places (where massaging is only a front for prostitution); the real deal will charge 250-400 baht for a typical two-hour massage and will often have a row of beefy farmers' daughters in white coats working on customers' feet in public view, while the other kind has wispy girls in evening dresses wearing too much make-up and saying "hello handsome" to every passing male. The current going rate for a 1 hour massage on Khao San Road is 220 baht.

Entertainment

Bangkok is a great place to go to the movies. Compared to the West, the cost of a ticket is a complete bargain at around 120 baht. Most cinemas have world-class standards and show the latest Hollywood and Thai releases. Watching Thai movies is a fun night out, as pretty much all of them have English subtitles. They are up to par with the latest technological innovations in the film industry, so expect to wear 3D glasses for some of the latest Hollywood releases, or visit the IMAX Theatre in Siam Paragon.

For non-mainstream cinema, House RCA (in Royal City Avenue) and APEX (in Siam Square) offer art films with English subtitles.

For other means of entertainment, Ratchadaphisek is a newly created entertainment paradise. Its bowling centres are of a superb standard with some of them resembling the inside of a nightclub. Dance while you play in style. Private karaoke lounges are usually connected to these bowling centres and are available at major hotels. There's even an ice skating rink and a top-class go-go kart track. As Ratchadaphisek is mostly aimed at the locals, you might want to go to similar venues in Siam Square or Sukhumvit. Musical, cabaret and theater entertainment by Thai performers can be found every night at the

Playhouse Theater] in the Asia Hotel which is connected to the Ratchathewi BTS station.

Horse Races are held on Sundays at two alternate turf clubs, the Royal Turf Club of Thailand in Dusit and the Royal Bangkok Sports Club on Henri Dunant Road (near Siam Square).

For something completely unique and fun travelers may wish to try Bangkok Bobble Football where you are literally wrapped in a plastic bubble and enjoy a game of soccer/football in a 5 a side format.

Festivals

➤ All of Thailand's major festivals are celebrated in Bangkok.

➤ **Chinese New Year Festival**. January or February. The obvious place to visit is Yaowarat, the Chinese district of Bangkok. Yaowarat Road is closed to cars and many stores and food stands crowd the road, with grandiose and colourful Chinese lion and dragon processions.

➤ **Songkran Festival**. 14-16 Apr. The traditional Thai New Year is an occasion for merriment all over the city, but most notably at Sanam Luang, near the Grand Palace, where the revered Phra Phuttha Sihing image is displayed and bathed by devotees. In the Wisut Kasat area, a Miss Songkran beauty contest is held and accompanied by merit-making and entertainment. Don't think it is particularly peaceful festival though; Khao San Road degenerates into a war zone as farangs and locals soak each other with super soakers

➤ **Royal Ploughing Ceremony.** May. Farmers believe that an ancient Brahman ritual, conducted at Sanam Luang, is able to forecast whether the coming growing season will be bountiful or not. The event dates back to the Sukhothai Kingdom. This ceremony was re-introduced in 1960 by His Majesty King Bhumibol Adulyadej and is considered the official commencement of the rice-growing season (and the rainy season). Nowadays, the ceremony is conducted by Crown Prince Maha Vajiralongkorn.

➤ **Loi Krathong** (ลอยกระทง). November. Loi Krathong is the Festival of Lights, and takes place on the evening of the full moon of the 12th month in the traditional Thai lunar calendar. In the western calendar this usually falls in November.

➤ **Trooping of the Colours.** December. Their majesties the King and Queen preside over this impressive annual event, held in the Royal Plaza near the equestrian statue of King Rama V in Dusit. Dressed in colourful uniforms, amid much pomp and ceremony, members of the elite Royal Guards swear allegiance to the King and march past members of the Royal Family.

➤ **HM The King's Birthday Celebrations.** December 5. On this day, Ratchadamri Road and the Grand Palace are elaborately decorated and illuminated. In the evening, hundred thousands of locals line the route from Sanam Luang to the Chitralada Palace to get a glimpse of the King when he is slowly chauffeur-driven past.

➢ **New Year Countdown Celebrations**. December 31. The most well-known and biggest countdown festival in Bangkok is held at Central World square in front of Central World. There are spectacular shows and live-on-stage concerts by popular singers and celebrities. After midnight, they celebrate with spectacular dazzling and colourful fireworks.

Cooking Class

➢ Cookly 6 Dish Cooking Experience & Local Market Tour in **Khao San**, NEW C.H. Guesthouse 85-87 Soi Ratche Damnoen Kiang Bavon niwat Pranakorn, +660899814871. ฿ 1,531.

Learn
Bangkok is one of South East Asia's educational hubs.

Study Abroad in Bangkok
The KUSEP-program (Kasetsart University Student Exchange Program) at Kasetsart University is an English program that offers courses from several different faculties for international students. Faculty of Economics and Faculty of Engineering have entire degree programs in English and, hence, the most courses taught in English are from these

two faculties. There are various elective courses on offer, too, that range from Thai language to Social Sciences and sports.

Siam University, Thailand's fifth oldest private university, also offers study abroad opportunities in Siam University's International Business Program(IBP). IBP is an undergraduate degree program taught in English and the participants are both Thai and international students. The program is business focused, i.e. most of the courses relate to Economics, Finance, Marketing, Management and Trade, but there are several courses from social sciences as well, from psychology to politics, law and languages. Exchange students at Siam University have plenty of options when making their course selections since they can pick their IBP courses freely; from the level and subject area that is most suitable and interesting for them. It is also possible to do a MBA degree or an exchange at Siam University.

Culinary studies
Thai cuisine is a favourite of many, and plenty of cooking schools provide half-day classes that provide a nice break from the day-to-day sightseeing monotony. Silom and Khao San Roadparticularly have some of the better-known Thai cooking schools.

> ➢ Cooking with Poo is one of the most highly acclaimed Thai cooking experiences in Bangkok, limited to 10 participants to maintain an intimate setting and includes a personal tour through the Klong Toey market to purchase ingredients for the

day's menu. The warm and fun class is hosted by Khun Poo, a long-time resident of the Klong Toey slum who's displayed amazing resolve despite personal difficulties and seeks to provide opportunities for other members of her community with much of the profit. Register in advance, she's often booked months in advance.

➤ Cooking for fun is one of the latest cookings schools that have joined. Limited to 6 participants per chef to ensure absolute enjoyment. Also includes a Market tour for those who choose to do the morning class. Located in the heart of Bangkok's oldest neighborhood Bang-Rak you will also find Bangkok's oldest surviving market. Go Thai Cooking School is located right inside the market to give you the authentic feel

Meditation

The essence of 'pure' Buddhism, can be practised at any temple in Thailand. In Bangkok however, there are also well-known centres that cater specifically to foreigners wishing to learn and practise. The International Buddhist Meditation Centre inside Wat Mahathat in Rattanakosin provides free meditation classes three times a day. If you can speak and understand the Thai language well enough, you may wish to go on your own retreat at a quiet temple on the outskirts of Bangkok. To pay for your stay, it is appreciated that you assist the resident monks on their morning alms rounds.

The Wat Pho temple in Rattanakosin offers well-regarded Thai massage courses. While aimed squarely at tourists, this is not necessarily a bad thing, as they're used to conducting classes in English.

Thai language schools
abound in Bangkok. Classes are attended by foreign aid workers, trust-fund babies seeking education visas, new residents, and retirees. Curriculum varies from school to school as do prices and time commitments.

> ➤ **RTL School** (โรงเรียนรักภาษาไทย), 888/104 Mahatun Plaza 10 Fl. (*BTS Phloen Chit, Mahatun Plaza Building, 10th fl.*), +66 2 255-3036, M-F 09:00-20:00. Rak Thai Language School opened in 2012 and uses the same Thai language teaching curriculum as the larger (and more expensive) UTL school. Courses are 3 hours in the mornings or afternoons, 5 days per week. Friendly teachers and fun atmosphere. RTL offers 5 speaking modules, 4 reading/writing modules, and other special topics which vary by month. 6,000 baht/month.

Buy
Many tourists find a 180 baht charge for a currency withdrawal from cash machines in Thailand - applied only to foreign bank cards - as an unpleasant surprise. If you are planning to exchange large sums, few offices of the SuperRich company consistently offer the top exchange

rates. To save time, consider the green K Excellence booth by the entry to the City Rail Train station at the Savarnabhumi airport.

Siam Square is the place to shop in Bangkok; the small sois of Siam Square have dozens of small designer boutiques. MBK Center is the most popular shopping malls for foreigners , as they sell fashion well below Western rates. Siam Paragon and the shopping plazas at Ratchaprasong are more popular to Thais. Ladies will also feel well at home in the Emporium in Sukhumvit.

Just take a few steps out of your hotel and Bangkok feels like a huge street market. Sukhumvit has the usual souvenirs, t-shirts and other tacky tourist junk. Browsing Khao San Road's roadside stalls is particularly good for clothing and accessories, many of them for a bargain. While many of these stalls still cater to the traditional hippie crowd, they have been slowly gentrifying to appeal a broader audience. The nearby Banglamphu Market sells cheap knock-offs of everything, just like the night markets in Silom and Rattanakosin.

In the weekends, the Chatuchak Weekend Market in Phahonyothin is a must as its 8,000 stalls together form the largest market in Southeast Asia. Shoppers can buy just about everything from clothing to potted plants and everything in between it is a paradise for browsers and bargain-hunters alike. A weekday alternative is Pratunam, one of the city's renowned garment markets. Clothes shopping here goes on wholesale, and you're even cheaper off if you buy in bulk. At Pantip

Plaza you can buy computer-related stuff from branded laptops to pirated DVDs. Just be aware that many of the "brand name" items are fakes/copies.

Yaowarat and Phahurat give a more authentic experience, although many stores sell the cheap teen accessories found elsewhere as well. Just sitting at a plastic chair and watching daily commerce evolve is a fun activity in itself. Phahurat is the best destination for fabrics, available in all colours and sizes. Pak Khlong Talat is a surprisingly fun wholesale market for all kinds of cut flowers and vegetables. If you're a morning person, visit it around 03:00, when new flowers from upcountry arrive and the marketplace is beautifully illuminated.

Thonburi, being one of the least developed areas of Bangkok, is the best place to experience what the city used to be like. A nice break from the pulsing city is the weekends-only Taling Chan Floating Market, which feels at least somewhat authentic as it blends a rural market with the canal side way of life. Beware though that the farang density is rising as the day progresses: This used to be a little untouched gem of a floating marked and the word has spread at the high speed of the internet... Wang Lang Market is an undiscovered gem with strictly local prices. The other side of the river, Rattanakosin, has everything a good Buddhist would need, be it amulets, monk bowls or human-sized Buddha statues.

For antiques, Silom is the place to go, as most potential buyers stay there in expensive hotels. River City in Yaowarat is the largest antique mall of the city, and priced to match. Gold and gems are popular buys, but be extremely wary as many tourists buy worthless pieces of cut glass believing it to be valuable gems. Never let a tuk-tuk driver convince you into a gem store, as more often than not, you're being ripped off. The same rule goes for tailoring shops; you can get a custom-made suit for amazingly cheap prices, but you have to know where to go, as many tailors provide bad quality see the box for advice on finding a good tailor.

If you want to shop and see the beautiful scene of Chaophraya River at night, Asiatique the riverfront is the largest waterfront themed and new lifestyle night shopping area. It is a combination of Thai history elements and modern lifestyle. It opens daily from 5pm to midnight. The easiest way to get there is via free shuttle boat near Saphan Taksin BTS station. It takes only ten minutes. Taxis are not recommended due to terrible traffic jams around here. Once you step off the boat, you will see an over 300 m long boardwalk along the river that looks like a romantic scene. There are a lot of shop here, you can find everything you would like both to eat and to buy. There are also entertainment shows; Calypso ladyboy cabaret and a classic Thai puppets performance. With retro props and buildings, it is also a good idea to take some photos at here.

Browsing second hand English-language books can best be done on Khao San Road. For new releases, there are plenty of chain stores in shopping plazas, including Asia Books, B2S, Bookazine and Kinokuniya. There's a particularly wide array of books on Asian culture and history; some have a good selection of foreign newspapers and magazines as well.

Getting money in Bangkok is relatively easy; credit cards are widely accepted and ATMs are spread all over the city, especially in downtown areas. They all charge 200 baht when using foreign ATM cards, except for Aeon which charges 150 baht. (Nov 2016: Citibank and HSBC might not charge as they didn't around 2014. See below for more information..

Be warned that Aeon ATMs will eat and destroy cards if anything goes wrong, such as entering in a wrong PIN one time (according to their helpline). Three of the most conveniently located Aeon ATMs can be found on Chakrapong street 170 m walk north from western end of Khao San Road on ground floor of Tang Hua Seng supermarket (logo with T in circle visible from distance) and in the central part of the second floor of MBK Center in Siam Squareand at the first floor of Central Department Store at Silom Complex in Silom. HSBC Thailand's branch is located at 968 Rama IV Road, in front of Lumphini Park and it's the only one location of HSBC ATM in Thailand. Citibank ATMs in Bangkok have 4 locations. There are contradicting reports about Aeon start charging a 150 baht fee from Jan 2014, although other people confirm they were not charged, same with Citibank ATM which should supposedly charge an ATM fee but there are reports in 2014 from BTS Sala Daeng ATM not charging the fee. Other option with Visa card would be go to branch of any Thai bank and withdraw money at window using cash advance which should be without any fees, but there are reports some clerks are lazy and refusing customers sending them to use ATM, when withdrawing using cash advance from your Visa card be careful about exchange rate which may be worse and your own bank cash advance fee.

Best to keep away from buying fake degrees from the Khao San Road as they are either not from a real university or cannot be verified.

"The Mall" in Bangkapi has a water park on the top floor. But, this huge mall does not have a map or directory located anywhere in the mall. All needs for directions must be asked at the information desk.

➢ Amphawa Floating Market. On Samutsongkram near Wat Amphawanjetiyaram. Amphawa Floating Market is one of the famous tourist attractions. Use bus number 76 and 967.

➢ Kwan-Reim floating market, +66 87 701-2878. Study the history of Bam Pen Nuer Temple and Bam Pen Tai Temple. New generation can see the past of people to illustrate offering some food to the monks, offering robes to Buddhist priests at monastery and listening to sermon. Number 27 and 503 buses on Sukhapiban 2 Rd. Second take number 113, 58, 113, 514 buses on Sukhapiban 3 Rd. These floating markets open Sa-Su 08:00-21:00 and holidays.

Eat

Bangkok boasts a stunning 50,000 places to eat; not only thousands of Thai restaurants, but a wide selection of world-class international cuisine too. Prices are generally high by Thai standards, but cheap by international standards; a good meal is unlikely to cost more than 300 baht, although there are a few restaurants (primarily in hotels) where you can easily spend 10 times this.

Sukhumvit by far has the best restaurants of Bangkok, though prices tend to be high. Practically every cuisine in the world is represented here, be it French, Lebanese, Mexican, Vietnamese, or fusion combining many of these together in a quirky, but delicious mix. Bangkok's Italian town is Soi Ton Sonnear Siam Square. Of course, for those on a budget, street stalls abound with simple Thai dishes at around 30 baht. There are especially plenty of budget restaurants in Khao San Road.

There are plenty of vegetarian restaurants in the more tourist-friendly parts of town (especially in hippie district Khao San Road). Vegetarian dishes are also readily available on the menus of regular restaurants.

On request, even typical street restaurants will easily cook a vegetarian equivalent of a popular Thai dish for you. Ask for "jay" food to leave the meat out of the dish. For example, "khao pad" is fried rice and "khao pad jay" is vegetarian fried rice. For vegans, the most common animal product used would be oyster sauce. To avoid it, say "mai ao naam man hoi". Be aware that all street noodle vendors use animal broth for noodle soup.

Don't miss out on a cold ice cream in hot Bangkok. Western chain stores Dairy Queen and Swensen's have booths in many malls and shopping centres. Or better yet, try an exotic fruit-flavoured ice cream at an Iberry shop. Their ice creams are tasty, cheap and safe to eat.

For Muslims, looking for Halal food, fortunately there is no problem. Most of KFCs sell Halal chicken. A lot of vendors on street food understand the term 'Halal' so it is always better to ask. A frown on their face on answering this question would indicate an absence of Halal Food. Tourists looking for Halal street food must disembark BTS at Ratchthewi station in direction of Phaya Thai and turn left on Petchaburi Road where lines of local Halal food outlets and cart food are located.

Dessert
Thai desserts are worth appreciating not only for their beauty but also their unique way of reflecting traditional culture. Most Thai desserts are quite sweet. Therefore, they are favoured both by Thai people and

foreigners. Real traditional desserts contain only 3 main ingredients; flour, sugar and coconuts. These ingredients are mixed by various methods such as boiling, steaming, frying, and grilling.

Tong Yip (ทองหยิบ), literally "Flower Egg Yolk Tart", is formed its shape as a flower. Its ingredient consists of egg yolk, sugar, and flower water boiled in sugar syrup. The word of "Thong" (ทอง) means gold represents reputation and prosperity. Thai people believe that gold will bring a good thing happens to their life. Thong Yip means Picking Gold. A nice Thong Yip will not smell of yolks and it has a sweet taste. You should buy it from markets and Thai dessert stores. The one of popular Thai dessert stores is Khanom Thai Baan Khanom Suay at Patthanakarn Road Soi 65.

Khanom Chan (ขนมชั้น), calls "Thai Jello", forms like a Jelly that is baked in 9 layers and set on a cookie pan. Its ingredient compounds of sugar, coconut milk, and flour are mixed. The word of "Khanom" (ขนม) means dessert or sweets, "Chan" (ชั้น) means layer or level that indicates to improve or increase in the state. Number nine in its layer is significant in affluence in Thai. Khanom Chan is popular because it has a sweet scent, a slightly oily thoroughly from increasing coconut milk and a smooth texture. You can get it from markets and Thai dessert stores. The popular store is Khanom Whan Mae Kwa (ขนมหวานแม่กวา) at Nangloeng Market.

Street food

While not particularly high class, street food is among the most delicious food and can be found all over Bangkok wherever you're staying, you rarely have to walk more than 100m for a cart of street restaurant.

Many street vendors sell satay (สะเต๊ะ) with hot sauce for 5-10 baht a piece.

One of Thailand's national dishes you can try is pad Thai (ผัดไทย), stir-fried rice noodles with eggs, fish sauce, tamarind juice and red chili pepper. It can be prepared for you on one of the ubiquitous carts, or in a street restaurant for about 50 baht. You can order it with chicken (gai) or shrimps (kung). Be aware that the pad Thai sold on the street on Khao San Road is changed to appeal to tourists, and is not an authentic pad Thai. Much better pad Thai is available in almost any restaurant on Khao San. A very authentic and cheap halal pad Thai is sold by on a cart at footsteps of pedestrian bridge on Petchaburi Road near BTS station Ratchathewi.

Another one of Thailand's national dishes you should try is tom yam kung (ต้มยำกุ้ง), a sour soup with prawns, lemongrass and galangal beware, as it is very spicy!

Khao man kai (ข้าวมันไก่) is another popular street food. You can identify it at stalls displaying boiled chicken. Served with a bowl of fragrant chicken soup is a mound of rice topped with sliced chicken pieces and cucumber. Side sauces are spicy and go well with the bland chicken and rice. You can sometimes add optional liver and gizzard if that is your taste.

If you like sweets, try to find a kanom roti (โรตี) street vendor. The crepe-like dessert is filled with sweetened condensed milk, lots of sugar, and can also have bananas inside. Also fun to watch them being made.

Khao San Road is known for its carts selling bugs yes, insects. They are deep fried, nutritious and quite tasty with the soy sauce that is sprayed on them. Types available: scorpions, water beetles, grasshoppers, crickets, bamboo larvae, mealworms and some more seasonal specialties. Break off the legs from grasshoppers and crickets or they will get stuck in your throat.

Ethnic cuisine
Thai dishes can roughly be categorised into central, northern, northeastern and southern cuisine. What's so great about Bangkok is that all these cuisines are present. Isaan food (from the northeast of Thailand) is a backpacker favourite; generally street restaurants serve on plenty of small plates that can be shared. Som tam (ส้มตำ) is a salad made from shredded and pounded raw papaya again, it is spicy, but oh so delicious. If you want to dine the Isaan way, also order some khao niew (sticky rice), kai yang (grilled chicken) and moo yang (grilled

pork). Isaan food is very spicy; say mai pet or pet nit noy to tone it down. Southern Thai cuisine is also worth it; many of them have congregated around Wang Lang in Thonburi. At least try the massaman curry (แกงมัสมั่น), it's delicious.

The place to go to for Chinese food is Yaowarat. It has a range of street stalls and cheap restaurants selling expensive delicacies at affordable prices. Soi Phadung Dao is the best street for huge seafood restaurants. Try 1 kg of huge barbecued prawns for about 300 baht. Phahurat, Bangkok's Little India, has some decent Indian restaurants.

Dinner cruises
Dinner cruises on the Chao Phraya River are a touristy (but fun) way of spotting floodlit temples while chowing down on seafood and watching Thai cultural performances. Most operate buffet-style and the quality of the food is so-so, but there's lots of it and it's not too spicy. While the river can give a romantic experience, it can also be dirty and smelly with lots of plants floating around.

Drinks and tips are usually not included in the listed prices below. Always make a reservation before heading out to the pier. There are many competing operators, most of them depart from the River City pier next to the Si Phraya Express Boat pier. Major operators include:

Chao Phraya Princess, 723 Supakarn Building, Charoen Nakhorn Rd, +66 2 860-3700. Departure 19:30. Large operator with four modern air-conditioned boats seating up to 250 people. Departure from River City pier. 1,300 baht.

Loy Nava, 1367 Charoen Nakhorn Rd, +66 2 437-4932,. Departure 18:00 or 20:10 daily. This dinner cruise heads out with 70-seater rice barges. Departure from Si Phraya pier (near River City), and there is a free pickup from most hotels. 1,400 baht.

Maeyanang, 183/59 Soi Chuchart-anusorn, Chaeng Watthana Rd, Nonthaburi, +66 2 659-9000. Departure 19:00 daily. Catered and operated by the Oriental Hotel, the Maeyanang is a custom-built ornately carved teakwood boat seating only 32 people, small enough to venture off the river down the subsidiary klongs. Departure from Oriental pier. 2,000 baht.

Manohra, 257 Charoen Nakhorn Rd, +66 2 477-0770,. Departure 19:30 daily. These restored Thai rice barges seat 40 people. Departure from Marriott Resort pier, with an optional pick-up from Saphan Taksin BTS station. 1,250-1,990 baht.

Wan Fah, 292 Rachawongse Rd, +66 2 222-8679. Departure 19:00 daily. These two-hour dinner cruises include a set meal of farang-friendly Thai food and seafood, live music and Thai classical dancing. Departure from River City. 1,000 baht.

Yok Yor Marina, 885 Somdet Chao Phraya Soi 17 +66 2 863-0565. Departure 20:00. Operated by the famous seafood restaurant, this is a much more local (and cheaper) option than the tourist cruises: pay a 160 baht "boat fee" and then order off the menu at normal restaurant prices. Departure from Yok Yor Marina on the Thonburi side of the river. There is a free shuttle service from Saphan Taksin BTS station.

Crostini @ Asiatique The Riverfront, Warehouse 6, Asiatique The Riverfront, Charoenkrung Rd.,, Wat Phraya Krai, Bang Kho Laem, Bangkok 10120, +66 2 639 3710 . OPEN 11.30AM -11.30PM.. Operated by the famous Italian Food Restaurant, Crostini Rooftop Italian Restaurant & Bar sits on a beautiful rooftop with a great view, and our newly renovated space is the perfect spot for a chill weekend. With everything prepared from scratch, expect nothing but fresh Italian cuisine and a few refreshing local twists on classic dishes.

Drink

Bangkok's nightlife is infamously wild, but it's not quite what it used to be: due to recent social order campaigns. Most restaurants, bars and clubs are now supposed to close at 02:00 AM, although quite a few stay open till much later. Informal roadside bars do stay open all night, particularly in Sukhumvitand Khao San Road. You must carry your passport for ID checks and police occasionally raid bars and clubs, subjecting all customers to drug tests and searches, though these mostly occur at places that cater for high society Thais rather than foreigners.

One of Bangkok's main party districts is Silom, home not only to perhaps the world's most famous go-go bar strip Patpong, but plenty of more legitimate establishments catering to all tastes. For a drink with a view, the open-air rooftop bars of Vertigo and Sirocco are particularly impressive. A large number of superhip and more expensive bars and nightclubs can be found in the higher sois of Sukhumvit, including, Q Bar, and Narz, as well as the hip area of Thong Lo (Soi 55).

Hippie hangout Khao San Road is also slowly gentrifying and a score of young artsy Thai teenagers have also made their mark there. Going out in Khao San Road is mostly casual, sitting at a roadside bar watching people pass by, but the Gazebo Club is a nightclub that stays open till the sun gets up. Most of the younger Thais prefer to congregate around Ratchadaphisek, home to the Royal City Avenue strip of nightclubs.

Smoking is forbidden in all restaurants, bars and nightclubs, whether air-conditioned or non-air-conditioned. Remarkably for Thailand, this rule is not strictly enforced.

Go-go and beer bars

The go-go bar is an institution of Bangkok's "naughty nightlife". In a typical go-go, several dozen dancers in bikinis (or less) crowd the stage, shuffling back and forth to loud music and trying to catch the eye of punters in the audience. Some (but not all) also put on shows where girls perform on stage, but these are generally tamer than you'd expect nudity, for example, is technically forbidden. In a beer bar, there are no stages and the girls are wearing street clothes.

If this sounds like a thinly veiled veneer for prostitution, it is. Although some point to the large number of American GIs during the Vietnam War as the point of origin of the Thai sex trade, others have claimed that current Thai attitudes towards sexuality have deeper roots in Thai history. Both go-go and beer bars are squarely aimed at the foreign touristsand it's fairly safe to assume that most if not all Thais in them are on the take. That said, it's perfectly OK to check out these shows without actually partaking, and there are more and more curious couples and even the occasional tour group attending. The main area is around Patpong in Silom, but similar bars to the ones at Patpong can be found in Sukhumvit, at Nana Entertainment Plaza (Soi 4) and Soi Cowboy (Soi 23). Soi 33 is packed with hostess bars, which are more upscale than the Soi Cowboy and Nana Plaza bars and do not feature go-go dancing. Before heading to these places, be sure to read the Stay safe section for some additional advice.

As go-go bars close around 01:00, there are so-called after-hour clubs that stay open till the sun gets up. They are not hard to find just hop in a taxi. Taxi drivers are eager to drive you there, as they get a hefty commission from club owners to bring you to them you might even get the ride for free. These clubs generally feel grim and edgy, and there are so-called "freelancers" among the girls (prostitutes). Some well-known after-hour clubs include ""Climax"" on Soi 11, Bossy Club in Pratunam, Spicy Club near Siam Square and the always famous Thermae on Sukhumvit between sois 15 and 17 in the basement underneath the Ruamchit short time hotel.

Gay nightlife
Thais are generally accepting of homosexuality and Bangkok has a very active gay nightlife scene, concentrated in Silom's Soi 2, Soi 4 and a short strip of gay go-go bars known as Soi Twilight (off Surawong Road). Gay strip bars all have free entry, but charge an extra 150 baht or so for drinks. The most popular gay drinking bars are The Balcony and Telephone Pub at Silom Soi 4, which are busy until 23:00. For the disco crowd, DJ Station and its late-night neighbour G.O.D. Club (located at Silom Soi 2) are packed every night beginning around 23:00. Between 17:00-22:00 over 200 men from around the world cruise, swim, dine and party at the nearby Babylon, considered by many to be the best gay sauna in the world. Babylon also has a budget and luxury accommodation.

All of these bars and clubs are aimed at gay men and the lesbian scene is much more low-key. Since the opening of full-time lesbian bars Zeta and E-Fun, a small lesbian community is starting to emerge along Royal City Avenue. Lesla (near Phahonyothin) is a lesbian bar that is opened on Saturday nights only. Bring along your passport for entrance age checking (they do not allow people under 20 years old).

Some Thai regulars in the gay nightlife scene skirt the fine line between partying and prostitution, and the Western visitor, being considered richer, is expected to pay any food and drink expenses and perhaps provide some "taxi money" in the morning. It's usually wise to ask a boy you pick up in a bar or club if he is after money, as it's not uncommon for them to start demanding money after sex. However most Thai boys looking for money for sex will refer to themselves as 'money boys' and as long as you ask them this with discretion its considered OK!.

Sleep

Bangkok has a vast range of accommodation, including some of the best hotels in the world and some of the worst dives too. Broadly speaking, Khao San Road is backpacker city; the riverside of Silom and Thonburi is home to The Oriental and The Peninsula respectively, often ranked among the best in the world (and priced to match). Most of the city's moderate and expensive hotels can be found in Siam Square, Sukhumvitand Silom, though they also have their share of budget options. UNDERSTAND:The Thai prpaganda has become very creative, trying to give you advise how to book a room for 1000 bath instead of 1500, omiting to mention the fact that 1000 bath is already scam. The ongoing room rates for whole Thailand including the islands are: Fan dorm 120-150; fan single room 200-300 for aircon add 50bath on top. Yes there are some rooms with exceptional views over Temples or rivers or bays, which are worth going up to 1000 bath for a double room with aircon and bathroom but these are exceptional rooms 1% of the offered accommodations. Generally everything over 500 bath is 99% scam.

When choosing your digs, think of the amount of luxury you want to pay for air-conditioning can be advised, as temperatures don't drop below 20°C at night. Also pay careful attention to Skytrain, metro and express boat access, as a well-placed station or pier could make your stay in Bangkok much more comfortable. In general, accommodation in Bangkok is cheap though. It's possible to have a decent double room with hot shower and air-conditioning for about 500 baht/night. If you want more luxury, expect to pay around 1,500 baht for a double room in downtown. Even staying at one of Bangkok's top hotels only sets you back around 5,000 baht the price of a standard double room in Europe.

One Bangkok hotel phenomenon of note is the guest fee of around 500 baht added to your bill if you bring along a newly found friend for the night. Some hotels even refuse Thai guests altogether, this is especially common in Khao San Road. These rules are obviously aimed at controlling local sex workers, which is why hotel security will usually hold onto your guest's ID card for the duration of the visit, but some hotels will also apply it to Western visitors or, more embarrassingly, try to apply it to your Thai partner. Look for the signs, or, if in doubt, ask the staff before check-in.

Stay safe

Given its size, Bangkok is surprisingly safe, with violent crimes like mugging and robbery unusual but you should be careful, of course. One of the biggest dangers is motorbikes who ride on pavements at speed, go through red lights, undertake buses as they stop to let passengers off and generally drive far too fast especially through stationary traffic. If you are going to hire a bike, make sure you have insurance in case you are injured. You may be the world's best driver but you'll meet many of the world's worst drivers in Thailand.

Bangkok does have more than its fair share of scams, and many individuals in the tourist business do not hesitate to overcharge unwary visitors. As a rule of thumb, it's wise to decline all offers made by someone who appears to be a friendly local giving a hapless tourist some local advice. Never get in a tuk-tuk if someone else is trying to get you into one. Most Bangkok locals do not approach foreigners without an ulterior motive.

It is illegal to talk badly of the king. Tourists, just like locals, will get arrested and serve extended jail terms if caught doing so. Be extremely careful if you choose to talk politics, and it's really better not to do so at all.

Scams

You should always be on the look-out for scammers, especially in major tourist areas. There are dozens of scams in Bangkok, but by far the most widely practised is the gem scam. Always beware of tuk-tuk drivers offering all-day tours for prices as low as 10 baht. You may indeed be taken on a full-day tour, but you will end up only visiting one gem and souvenir shop after another. Don't buy any products offered by pushy salesmen the "gems" are pretty much always worthless pieces of cut glass and the suits are of deplorable quality. The tuk-tuk driver gets a commission if you buy something and fuel coupons even if you don't. Unless the idea of travelling by tuk-tuk appeals to you, it's almost always cheaper, more comfortable and less hassle to take a metered taxi.

In general, never ask a taxi driver for a recommendation for something. They will very likely take you to a place where they get a commission, and be of dubious quality. In particular, do not ask a taxi driver for a restaurant recommendation. An infamous place taxi drivers take unsuspecting tourists is Somboon D which is a terrible seafood restaurant in a seedy area under the train tracks on Makkasan Rd. A typical meal there costs 800 baht per person and it comes with little seafood, no service, and complaints are not taken by management. Instead of asking a taxi driver, search the web, ask a local on the street, or just walk around -- you will surprise yourself with what is around a corner in Bangkok.

Be highly skeptical when an English-speaking Thai at a popular tourist attraction approaches you *out of the blue*, telling that your intended destination is *currently closed* or offering discount admissions. Temples are almost always free (the main exceptions are Wat Phra Kaew and Wat Pho) and open just about every day of the year. Anyone telling you otherwise, even if they have an official-looking identification card, is most likely out to scam you, especially if they suggest a tuk-tuk ride to some alternate sights to see until the sight re-opens. At paid admission sites, verify the operating hours at the ticket window.

If you entered one of these tuk-tuks, touts often will drop you off at a certain place, such as a genuine Buddhist temple. Here you will find a man that claims to be an official, and he guides you in a certain direction. There you will find another "official" who also claims that a certain attraction is closed. This way, a tourist hears the same statement by multiple people, and is more eager to believe that his or her intended destination indeed is closed. Never get involved with these scammers or believe any of their statements.

Another scam is for a friendly Thai person to approach a tourist and provide a set of recommended locations to visit, including at least one shop, and even volunteer to mark them on your map and negotiate a fair tuk tuk price to take you to these destinations. At the first location, typically a nice, off the beaten path temple, a man praying will strike up a conversation and ask you where you're going. Upon seeing the store on your itinerary, he will reaffirm the quality and assure you he buys from there regularly. These stories can be incredibly detailed, and include cell phone pictures or even receipts. These men are not unbiased though, but part of an elaborate scheme, working with the first man to get you to buy marked up gems or poor quality suits. The temples can be worth checking out, but do not buy anything!

When getting a taxi, it is a good idea to hail a moving taxi from the main road, or to walk a short distance out of a major tourist area before looking for one. This is no guarantee of honesty, but greatly increases your chances of finding an honest driver, of which there are plenty in Bangkok, even if it sometimes seems that every driver is on the make. Most of the untrustworthy drivers are the ones standing still in tourist areas. Another important rule of thumb is to insist on the meter for taxis and agree on a price in advance for tuk-tuks. If they refuse, or quote silly prices, just walk out and get a different one as they're rarely in short supply. The Thai phrase to ask a driver to use the meter is mee-TOE, khap if you're male and mee-TOE, kha if you're female.

Beware of tuk-tuk or taxi drivers who approach you speaking good English or with an " farang" sign, especially those who mention or take you to a tailor shop (or any kind of business). They are paid by inferior tailor shops to bring tourists there to be subjected to high pressure sales techniques. If at any point your transportation brings you somewhere you didn't intend or plan to go, walk away immediately, ignore any entreaties to the contrary, and find another taxi or tuk-tuk.

Beware of a very overweight Western woman who approaches you with a story about how her luggage has just been stolen and needs money to get home. For several years now, she has usually lurked around the tourist attractions in Bangkok looking for prey. The scam industry in Bangkok is large enough to employ farangs!

Also beware of a woman who goes by the name of Koiy who runs a travel tour company named Tourist Information Tour Co., Ltd which operates under the Licence Number 12/01451. Her offices are located at 7101 Ka-om Rd., Wat Som Subdist, Pomprab Dist., Bangkok. For several years she has had locals, who are fluent in English, approach tourists to give "advice" on a government run tour agency that is used by locals because the prices are so low. They will claim that it is the only government agency and may claim that you will receive a (student, business, tourist...) discount of up to 20%. At first you will only be significantly overcharged, but if multiple trips are booked at one time the later portions of your trip may not be booked at all and you will be left stranded.

Also beware of private bus companies offering direct trips from Bangkok to other cities with "VIP" buses. There are a lot of scams performed by these private bus companies. The so-called direct VIP trips may end up changing three or four uncomfortable minibuses to the destination, and the 10-11 hour trip may well turn into 17-18 hours. Instead, try to book public BKS buses from the main bus terminals. It's worth the extra shoe-leather, as there have been reports of robberies on private buses as well.

As of 2012, there is a scam involving the local police and marijuana. If you attempt to purchase marijuana from one of the taxi or tuk-tuk drivers on Kao San Rd., there is the potential that you will get ripped off by the police. The scam goes like this: you ask for the weed, and the driver will tell you he knows a friend who he will call. The friend will show up and take you in the tuk-tuk to do the marijuana/money exchange. You'll get some terrible quality stuff and then get dropped off. Immediately after being dropped off, local police will run up on you and search you, finding the marijuana. Then, you'll be forced to go to the station with them and bribe. The going rate is USD1,000 but you could bargain down to USD600. They will walk you to the ATM and watch you withdraw the money, which you then hand over as your "fee" to go free. It's an awful scam. Don't try to buy marijuana in Bangkok unless you know what you're doing.

Go-go bars

Bangkok is known for its go-go bars and the prostitution that comes along with it. Technically, some aspects of prostitution are illegal (eg. soliciting, pimping), but enforcement is rare, and brothels are common. It's not illegal to pay for sex or to pay a "bar fine" (a fee the bar collects if you want to take an employee away).

The age of consent in Thailand is 15, but a higher minimum age of 18 applies in the case of prostitutes. Penalties for sex with minors are harsh. All adult Thais must carry an identity card, which will state that they were born in 2534 or earlier if they were over the age of 18 on 1 January 2010 (in the Thai calendar, 2010 is the year 2553). Many hotels retain the ID cards of prostitutes for the duration of their visit. Whilst most prostitutes are employed by bars or similar businesses, some are "freelancers". Petty theft and other problems are more common with these freelancers. HIV and AIDS awareness is better than it used to be, but infection statistics among entertainment industry workers remain high; freelancers are the highest risk group. Almost all girls insist on using condoms.

While walking in go-go bar areas is generally safe, you have to be cautious of touts who try to drag you into the Patpong upstairs bars with offers of ping-pong shows and 100-baht beer. The beer may well be 100 baht, but the "show" you'll be treated to will be 1,000 baht or more. A good idea is to let your friend check the place with you waiting outside (and if he doesn't come out in a few minutes you should call the police) and don't interact with workers during show, don't drink anything offered, don't let some friendly Thai sit next to you and talk to you, because you will end up paying for everything mentioned. If you follow this advice you can see ping pong show for 200 baht without paying anything else, just the ticket to bar.

Fights

Do not get into fights with locals. Thais are peace loving people, but when a Thai fights a foreigner, it is never a fair fight. You'll wind up having to fight 10-20 others who were not initially involved, or the police will be called and not do anything to assist you (especially the metropolitan police, as they normally have very limited English skills; always contact the Tourist Police (telephone 1155) when in trouble). Thais are also notorious for fighting with weaponry (guns, knives, broken bottles, metal rods) or employing Muay Thai techniques. These are usually produced from their concealed locations, with foreigners getting seriously injured or worse. Just avoid all confrontations. If you do get involved in a situation, it is better to apologise and get the heck out of there. In Thailand, discretion is definitely the better part of valour.

Animal abuse and Wildlife Trafficking

Elephants are a large part of Thailand's tourist business, and the smuggling and mistreatment of elephants for tourist attractions is a widespread practice. Be aware that elephants are often separated from their mothers at a young age to be cruelly trained under captivity for the rest of their lives. Discourage this kind of treatment by refusing to participate in elephant rides or any other animal-based entertainment.

A once depressingly common sight on the congested streets of Bangkok is elephant begging, which has significantly decreased in recent years due to police enforcement. During night hours, mahouts (trainers) with lumbering elephants approach tourists to feed the creatures bananas or take a photo with them for a fee. The elephants are brought to the city to beg in this way because they are out of work and are mistreated and visibly distressed under the conditions of the city. Please avoid supporting this cruelty by rejecting the mahouts as they offer you bananas to feed the elephants.

Due to its location, lax laws, and resources, many illegal animal products come through Bangkok. Rare and endangered species are often sold at markets for pets (especially at Chatuchak), and many other animal products are sold as luxury items. Avoid buying rare pets, leather, ivory, talons, dried sea creatures (such as starfish), fur, feathers, teeth, wool, and other products since they are most likely the result of illegal poaching, and buying them contributes greatly to animal endangerment and abuse. Bringing these items into the United States is a federal crime. Most countries have similar laws because endangered species are protected by CITES. Report illegal wildlife trade with the app Wildlife Witness; be part of the solution!

Food and water
As elsewhere in Thailand, be careful with what you eat. Outside of major tourist hotels and resorts, stay away from raw leafy vegetables, egg-based dressings like mayonnaise, unpackaged ice cream and minced meat as hot weather tends to make food go bad faster. In short, stick to boiled, baked, fried or peeled food.

Tap water in Bangkok is said to be safe when it comes out the plant, but unfortunately the plumbing along the way often is not, so it's wise to avoid drinking the stuff, even in hotels. Any water served to you in good restaurants will at least be boiled, but it's better to order sealed bottles instead, which are available everywhere at low prices.

In some areas, like the smaller sois surrounding Khao San Road, there are coin-operated filtration machines, allowing you to refill your drink bottles with safe water. These vending machines are often seen being used by locals, so they should be relatively safe.

Take care with ice, which may be made with tap water of questionable potability as above. Some residents claim that ice with round holes is made by commercial ice makers who purify their water; others state that it is wise not to rely on that claim.

Contact

Internet

Internet cafés abound in Bangkok. You'll generally be looking at rates of around 30-60 baht per hour in tourist-laden districts like Khao San Road, 20-30 baht per hour in downtown (the top floors of MBK for example), and 10-15 baht per hour if you would venture into residential areas (where the speed generally is still high).

An increasing number of cafés and pubs offer free Wi-Fi to their customers, including the ubiquitous Coffee World chain in all of its branches (ask for the password at the counter). TrueMove offers both free and paid Wi-Fi access. If you want to get online for free, you must register first, and both session and overall time is limited. Their network is accessible in many malls, including Siam Square, and sometimes can be available from your room if you stay in a nearby hot-spot just look for the 'truewifi' network, you can register right there. Most hotels and guest houses provide at least some form of Internet. Some have Wi-Fi access inside the rooms but inquire before booking.

There is not a lot of free Wi-Fi available in old districts like Rattanakosin or Yaowarat.

Telephone

The area code for Bangkok is **02**. You only need to dial the 0 if you're calling from within Thailand. Pay phones are not commonplace, as most Thais have a mobile phone. If you want to avoid high roaming costs, you can buy a tourist SIM card for 299 baht at Suvarnabhumi Airport (or other mobile phone stores throughout the city). The 299 baht is not just for the SIM card, but is immediately your first pre-paid amount. Topping it up is easy; Topup online, at a kiosk or just walk into a 7-Eleven convenience store and pick an amount you want to add.

Post

Bangkok's red post boxes are found all over the city. There are also plenty of Thailand Post offices around for sending post and packages. In tourist areas, there are post offices in the Khao San Road area (in front of Wat Bowonniwet) and at Sukhumvit Road (between Soi 4 and 6).

If you're staying in Bangkok for a longer time, you might want to make use of *poste restante*, so other people can send you letters or parcels using a post office's address. Post offices keep the letters for at least two months. Letters sent via *poste restante* must have the receiver's name on it, with the family name in underlined capital letters. If you want to pick them up near Khao San Road (opposite Wat Bowonniwet), it must be addressed to Poste Restante, Banglamphubon Post Office, Bangkok, 10203, Thailand. If you want to pick up your post in the Sukhumvit area, make sure it is addressed to

Poste Restante, Nana Post Office, Sukhumvit Road, Bangkok, 10112, Thailand.

Cope

Medical tourism

The word is out on the quality and value of Thailand's healthcare, and the numbers of visitors coming has increased accordingly. Patients have come to love the sparkling modern facilities with all the latest equipment, the highly professional doctors and medical staffs many with Western certification, and especially the gentle nature and famous Thai service touch they receive everywhere in Thailand.

Many travellers go to Bangkok to undergo medical treatments at a fraction of the cost charged in their home countries. The best-regarded (and most expensive) is Bumrungrad Hospital, which attracts about 400,000 foreign patients per year or an average of 1,000+ a day. Other hospitals, such as Samitivej also specialize in serving foreigners. Private hospitals in Thailand are accredited by the government according to international standards, and many of the doctors in Thailand hold international accreditation and relevant licences.

Thailand was the first country in Southeast Asia to receive JCI accreditation, and many of Bangkok's hospitals have won international awards and are internationally accredited. [source6] Thailand's 21 JCI-accredited hospitals (as of August 2013) are: Bangkok Heart Hospital,

Bangkok Hospital, Dr. Sunil Dental Clinic, Bangkok International Dental Center, BNH Hospital, Bumrungrad International, Central General Hospital, Chaophya Hospital, Metta International Eye Center (Ambulatory Care), Navamin 9 Hospital, Nonthavej Hospital, Praram 9 Hospital, Ramkhamhaeng Hospital, Saimai Hospital, Samitivej Srinakarin Hospital, Samitivej Sukhumvit Hospital, Sikarin Hospital, Synphaet Hospital, Vejthani Hospital, Vibhavadi Hospital, Wattanosoth Cancer Hospital and Yanhee Hospital.

The Clinical Care Program Certification (CCPC) includes 15 categories of clinical services for certification; the following 5 Thailand hospitals have received certificates from the Joint Commission International (JCI) for CCPC in the following areas:

Bangkok Hospital Medical Center

1. Acute Myocardial Infarction Program
2. Breast Cancer Program
3. Diabetes Mellitus (Type 2)
4. Heart Failure Program
5. Low Back Pain Program
6. Primary Stroke Center

Bumrungrad International

1. Acute Myocardial Infarction Program

2. Chronic Kidney Disease Stage I to IV Program

3. Diabetes Mellitus Type 1 and 2 Program

4. Primary Stroke Program

Samitivej Srinakarin Hospital

1. Childhood Asthma

2. Low Back Pain program

3. Primary Stroke program

Samitivej Sukhumvit Hospital

1. Acute Myocardial Infarction Program

2. Lung Cancer Program

3. Osteoarthritis of the Knee Program

Vejthani Hospital

1. Diabetic Care

2. Heart Failure

3. Knee Replacement

Popular treatments, ranging from cosmetic, organ transplants and orthopaedic treatments to dental and cardiac surgeries, are available at a price much lower than the US or Europe. For example, Bumrungrad Hospital charges 90,000 baht for an all-inclusive breast implant package. Bangkok is also well-known as a centre for sexual reassignment surgery for people wishing to change their physical sex, although this falls out of the scope of a casual vacation.

Dental and medical clinics are everywhere in Bangkok; one can hardly walk ten minutes without seeing signs for doctors and dentists. They range from small one-chair clinics to entire buildings devoted solely to dental treatment. One such place is Bangkok International Dental Center (BIDC), which employs some 80 dentists with over 120 highly-trained and experienced staff. BIDC was the first dental centre in Thailand to be awarded JCI accreditation, the gold standard of medical certification. Despite the global standards and latest equipment, prices still make one smile at 50-70% less for comparable treatments in Western countries.

On the dental side, popular procedures are available most everywhere, including teeth whitening, dental implants, and orthodontics. For those searching for skin-care treatments, look no further: Bangkok offers scores of dermatology clinics and a multitude of procedures and treatments.

There are many dental clinics with English-speaking dentists and staff. The largest of them is the Bangkok International Dental Center (*BIDC*) with branches in Ratchadaphisek and Siam Square. There are also plenty of teeth whitening, implant and orthodontic providers over town.

Dr. Sunil Dental Clinic is located at Sukhumvith Soi 71, Soi Predee Panomyong 14, Building No.5, Moobaan Pakamas, Bangkok, Thailand 10250, For BTS: Phrakhanong station (#E8), They provide a wide range of dental services such as laser teeth whitening, dental implants, crown/porcelain veneers and bridges within 24 hours, bonding, gum lifts, aesthetic dentures and tooth colour fillings.

Bangkok is an ideal place to get your travel vaccinations. The Queen Saovabha Memorial Institute provide red cross sealed immunizations for much cheaper than most other countries. Vaccinations that would have cost over USD500 in North America may cost less than USD30.

The Thai Red Cross Anonymous Clinic on Ratchadamri Road (approximately 5 minutes walk from BTS Ratchadamri, towards Silom) provides low cost sexual health services for those in need. It has English speaking doctors, HIV test results within the hour (200 baht), and a dispensary for medications to treat other venereal diseases. It is busy so be prepared for a wait. Donations are greatly appreciated, there is a large box near the exit for this purpose.

Top things to do in Bangkok

The Grand Palace in Bangkok

If there is one must-see sight that no visit to Bangkok would be complete without, it's the dazzling, spectacular Grand Palace, undoubtedly the city's most famous landmark. Built in 1782 - and for

150 years the home of the Thai King, the Royal court and the administrative seat of government - the Grand Palace of Bangkok is a grand old dame indeed, that continues to have visitors in awe with its beautiful architecture and intricate detail, all of which is a proud salute to the creativity and craftsmanship of Thai people. Within its walls were also the Thai war ministry, state departments, and even the mint. Today, the

The Grand Palace
Within the palace complex are several impressive buildings including Wat Phra Kaew (Temple of the Emerald Buddha), which contains the small, very famous and greatly revered Emerald Buddha that dates back to the 14th century.

The robes on the Buddha are changed with the seasons by HM The King of Thailand, and forms an important ritual in the Buddhist calendar. Thai Kings stopped living in the palace around the turn of the twentieth century, but the palace complex is still used to mark all kinds of other ceremonial and auspicious happenings.

Grand Palace Layout and Orientation
The palace complex, like the rest of Ratanakosin Island, is laid very similar to the palaces of Ayutthaya, the glorious former capital of Siam which was raided by the Burmese. The Outer Court, near the entrance, used to house government departments in which the King was directly involved, such as civil administration, the army and the treasury. The

Temple of the Emerald Buddha is located in one corner of this outer court. The Central Court is where the residence of the King and halls used for conducting state business were located. Only two of the throne halls are open to the public, but you'll be able to marvel at the exquisite detail on the facades of these impressive structures.

The Inner Court is where the King's royal consorts and daughters lived. The Inner Court was like a small city entirely populated by women and boys under the age of puberty. Even though no royalty currently reside in the inner court, it is still completely closed off to the public. Despite the proximity of the Grand Palace and Wat Phra Kaew, there's a distinct contrast in style between the very Thai Temple of the Emerald Buddha and the more European inspired design of the Grand Palace (the roof being the main exception). Other highlights are Boromabiman Hall and Amarinda Hall, the original residence of King Rama I and the Hall of Justice.

Important Note about the Grand Palace:
A strict dress code applies. The Grand Palace with The Temple of the Emerald Buddha is Thailand's most sacred site. Visitors must be properly dressed before being allowed entry to the temple. Men must wear long pants and shirts with sleeves (no tank tops. If you're wearing sandals or flip-flops you must wear socks (in other words, no bare feet.) Women must be similarly modestly dressed. No see-through clothes, bare shoulders, etc. If you show up at the front gate

improperly dressed, there is a booth near the entrance that can provide clothes to cover you up properly (a deposit is required).

About Wat Phra Kaew

Wat Phra Kaew or the Temple of the Emerald Buddha (officially known as Wat Phra Sri Rattana Satsadaram) is regarded as the most important Buddhist temple in Thailand. Located in the historic centre of Bangkok, within the grounds of the Grand Palace, it enshrines Phra Kaew Morakot (the Emerald Buddha), the highly revered Buddha image meticulously carved from a single block of jade. The Emerald Buddha (Phra Putta Maha Mani Ratana Patimakorn) is a Buddha image in the meditating position in the style of the Lanna school of the north, dating from the 15th century AD

Royal Reception Halls

Nowadays its impressive interior is used for important ceremonial occasions like coronations. It also contains the antique throne, used before the Western style one presently in use. Visitors are allowed inside the spacious European style reception room or Grand Palace Hall (Chakri Maha Prasat). Then there's the impressive Dusit Hall, rated as perhaps the finest architectural building in this style, and a museum that has information on the restoration of the Grand Palace, scale models and numerous Buddha images.

The Grand Palace

Opening Hours: Daily 08:30 - 15:30

Location: Na Phra Lan Road, Old City (Rattanakosin)
Price Range: Tickets sold from 8:30 - 15:30 and cost 500 baht! One ticket includes entry to Vimanmek Palace and Abhisek Dusit Throne Hall

Wat Arun in Bangkok

Wat Arun, locally known as Wat Chaeng, is situated on the west (Thonburi) bank of the Chao Phraya River. It is easily one of the most stunning temples in Bangkok, not only because of its riverside location, but also because the design is very different to the other temples you can visit in Bangkok. Wat Arun (or temple of the dawn) is partly made up of colourfully decorated spires and stands majestically over the water.

Wat Arun is almost directly opposite Wat Pho, so it is very easy to get to. From Sapphan Taksin boat pier you can take a river boat that stops at pier 8. From here a small shuttle boat takes you from one side of the river to the other for only 3 baht. Entry to the temple is 100 baht. The temple is open daily from 08:30 to 17:30.

We would recommend spending at least an hour visiting the temple. Although it is known as the Temple of the Dawn, it's absolutely stunning at sunset, particularly when lit up at night. The quietest time to visit, however, is early morning, before the crowds.

Given beauty of the architecture and the fine craftsmanship it is not surprising that Wat Arun is considered by many as one of the most beautiful temples in Thailand. The spire (prang) on the bank of Chao Phraya River is one of Bangkok's world-famous landmarks. It has an imposing spire over 70 metres high, beautifully decorated with tiny pieces of coloured glass and Chinese porcelain placed delicately into intricate patterns.

You can climb the central prang if you wish, the steps are very steep but there is a railing to balance yourself. Getting up is as tricky as getting down! When you reach the highest point you can see the winding Chao Phraya River and the Grand Palace and Wat Pho opposite. Along the base of this central tower there are sculptures of Chinese soldiers and animals.

Head into the ordination hall and you can admire a golden Buddha image and the detailed murals that decorate the walls. Although Wat Arun is a very popular for tourists, it is also an important place of worship for Buddhists. Make sure you dress appropriately, or pick up one of the cover ups that are for rent near the entrance.

History

Wat Arun was envisioned by King Taksin in 1768. It is believed that after fighting his way out of Ayutthaya, which was taken over by a Burmese army at the time, he arrived at this temple just as dawn was breaking. He later had the temple renovated and renamed it Wat

Chaeng, the Temple of the Dawn. It used to be the home of the Emerald Buddha, before the capital and Palace was moved to the other side of the river. This can now be seen at the Grand Palace.

The central prang was extended during the reign of Rama III (between 1824 and 1851), and is now one of the most visited sites in Thailand. It was also Rama III who added the decoration of the spires with porcelain, so that they glimmer in the sunshine.

Wat Arun

Opening Hours: 08:00 -17:30
Location: Located on the west side of Chao Praya River (opposite Tha Thien Pier)
Price Range: 50 Baht

Bangkok Floating Markets

Even though transactions are more concerned with tourists rather than locals these days, the floating market;boats are still piled high with tropical fruit and vegetables, fresh, ready-to-drink coconut juice and local food cooked from floating kitchens located right on the boat.

To enjoy the atmosphere without haggling over prices, try relaxing on a guided boat tour of Damnoen Saduak market. Floating markets are Taling Chan Market, Bang Ku Wiang Market, Tha Kha, and Damnoen Saduak.

Khlong Lat Mayom Floating Market

Khlong Lat Mayom is one of the three floating markets located close to Bangkok, no more than twenty kilometres from town and accessible by taxi from Wongwian Yai (the last BTS station on the Silom Line). Khlong Lat Mayom is nothing like the huge touristy Damnoen Saduak or the crowded Amphawa but really has the charm and authenticity of a local market and you might be one of the only foreigners around. You can spend a couple of hours here then move to the largest Taling Chan floating market, just a couple of kilometers away.

Everybody love floating markets - Thai and tourists alike - you just have to see how locals flock to the place on weekends! Local market culture has deep roots in Thai daily life and eating out is not a special event as it is in western culture: it's fun, cheap and casual, and Thai food has so many variations it can be a travelling theme on its own.

Just like the two other markets around bangkok, the definition of 'floating market' is a bit stretched, the place being in fact more of a riverside market. The canal here is very narrow and only few boats are parked all alongside the riverbank and below a low bridge, cooking for customers who sit at low tables all along the water. Eating is always the highlight of a floating market visit, sitting on a little wooden stool not higher than 10 cm and ordering a dish cooked on a tiny wooden boat anchored just next to your table is such a fun and exotic experience!

Don't be shy and try some of the dishes you are not familiar with... if you don't know what it is, just point at your neighbour's plate: noodle soups, Pad Thai, Kanom Jeen (cold rice vermicellis) or Hoi Tod (oyster omelet) for 20 to 30 baht per plate. The drinks are usually sold by another person walking around.

The largest part of the market is built on firm ground and is surprisingly large and fun. One side is dedicated to the fresh market, mostly beautiful veggies and fruits, while the other side sells all kinds of colorful snacks, sweets and cooked food. You can find familiar or surprising tropical fruits: huge papayas, large green or ripe mangoes, chompoo and sapodillas, massive pomelos like overgrown grapefruits. If you think you know pineapple and bananas, try again! If it's your first time in tropical county, you will be surprised, it's nothing like what you have tried in your country.

Further into the market is where you can buy cheap clothing, house decoration, accesories, toys and the unavoidable flowers and plants, two items always popular at riverside markets. If you have kids, take them for a pony ride at the ranch just down the road; they will ride their cute little friend from the ranch to the market and back, definitely a great memory for them and a great photo for you.

To make the best of your morning, it might be a good idea to combine both Taling Chan and Khlong Lat Mayom as they are only a couple of kilometers away from each other. Start with Khlong Lat Mayom first as it is the smallest of both, then move to Taling Chan where you can board a longtail boat for a very small fee and ride around the neighboring khlongs. Both should give you a great insider's view of the daily life of river people and a great morning away from town - and you won't have to wake up before sunrise to enjoy it!

Damnoen Saduak Floating Marke

Damnoen Saduak is the most popular floating market in Thailand, great for photo opportunities, food, and for giving you an insight into a bygone way of life. An early morning start is worth it to avoid the heat and catch Damnoen Saduak at its liveliest. Most visitors who come to Thailand want to visit a floating market and many of them will end up here. Don't let that put you off though, it's an enjoyable morning out of the city and if you avoid the tourist shops you can get a real sense of the place. The market is over an hour outside Bangkok, and the easiest way to get there is to join a tour.

The bus leaves Bangkok just after 07:00. Our chatty and cheerful guide gives us a potted history of Thailand and points out the interesting sites as we whizz out into the provinces. High rises are quickly replaced by salt farms and lush countryside. First stop is an Orchid Farm and coconut producer. It is impressive how many uses there are for coconuts and the small workshop has managed to turn the entire tree into a business, young shoots boiled for palm sugar, squeezed for oil, lampshades, ladders, and even fuelling their fires with the husks. Next to this hive of activity (beware of the sugar-hungry bees) the orchids seem less exciting, but it is still beautiful to see them in their natural habitat, especially if you are used to seeing them on window-sills in plastic tubs.

After this brief stop, it's only a ten-minute drive to the pier to hop onto decorated long-tail boats that are waiting to take you to the market. The roar of the engine disturbs the quiet as the boat glides down the narrow canals, small wooden houses on stilts fringe the banks, some with larger ponds than lawns. The boat driver slows down to let you appreciate the winding waterways and get a brief glimpse of those who live on the river. The journey takes around 20 minutes and it's great to enjoy the peace before the hectic pace of the market. It may feel overcrowded at first glance, but visitors and sellers bring noise and colour to the area.

Stepping off the boat, you find yourself amongst the busy stalls selling similar products to those you can find at Chatuchak weekend market, small toy elephants, tiger balm and the compulsory 'I was here' T-shirts. It's not surprising to find this at the most famous floating market in Thailand and it can feel a little commercialised but if you walk further, you will find the food-sellers, who not only look more photogenic, but also have some far tastier goods. Unlike most of the other floating markets, the popularity of Damnoen Saduak attracts many fruit sellers rowing their boats along the narrow canals, meaning that you're guaranteed great pictures. There is plenty of tasty food to try along the docks, from freshly-made mini coconut pancakes to boat noodles in their rich meaty broth.

We were given plenty of time to wander around, taste some local produce and take plenty of pictures. Damnoen Saduak is the most popular market for a good reason; it guarantees the floating market experience, even if it doesn't always feel authentic.

Amphawa Floating Market

Amphawa is the second most popular floating market near Bangkok, not as large as Damnoen Saduak but more authentic, with visitors almost exclusively Thai. Located 50 km from Bangkok this once small village was apparently already present in the mid-Seventeenth Century. It has become such a magnet for Thai weekenders that food stalls have grown from the riverbanks and stretched far into the surrounding streets.

The main draw is of course eating seafood grilled procariously on wooden boats moored around the famous central bridge, serving an appetizing array of huge prawns, shellfish and squid. From noon until late in the evening, the smell is simply irresistible and customers flock to each side of the river all day long.

Seafood prices are what you would expect at floating markets: according to weight, but to give you an idea, five large prawns usually cost 300 baht. Customers perch on rows of narrow steps leading down to the water and food is brought directly from the boats onto really tiny tables. If you don't feel like sitting on a concrete ledge very close to brownish waters, walk a bit further from the bridge to find restaurants with real tables and chairs. Even better, try to get a seat on the balcony of the restaurant next to the bridge, it's the only one around but you might have to wait a bit or come early. The nicest and most quiet restaurant is located at the very end of the broadwalk where the canal meets the Mae Khlong River.

All along each side of the canal, old charming wooden shops sell Amphawa souvenirs, from the obvious T-shirt to some more interesting creations, and of course lots of sweets, snacks and ice cream - Thai people have a very sweet tooth and a passion for nibbling all day. In all streets radiating from the market you can find an incredible array of local food sold from small carts during the weekend only. Most food looks familiar but some really look unusual or even funny, from ice cream sandwiches to alien-looking helmet crab egg salad (Yum Magda Talay).

Once you have had enough walking (or trying to walk) around Amphawa, it's time to take one of the many longtail boats and explore the surrounding canals and rivers. It's not as impressive as the

Bangkok Khlongs but it's always good fun, and after the heat of the market the breeze from the river is a welcome relief. Two tours are available from the many counters found around the bridge: the temple tour and the island tour. Both usually coast 50 baht per person for joined tours and 500 baht for a private boat. 50 baht appears cheap but the tour last a lot longer as the boat has to wait to be full to leave then wait for all passengers at each stop.

On the other side of the Mae Khlong River, Amphawa hides a very surprising temple called Wat Bang Koong, which you definitely shouldn't miss if you came all the way from Bangkok. The boat takes you first to a couple of temples, that are rather small but each have their own personality, such as surprisingly large golden seated buddhas, tall chedis and even small museum houses. It's not all that impressive but it's a good change from the crowds at Amphawa.

The true highlight of the cruise is Wat Bang Koong... built in the middle of nowhere, this temple alone is worth the trip to Amphawa. Of course kids and teenagers love the wacky mini zoo set on the temple grounds - a camel, an ostrich, a dozen deer and a group of boars, a couple of naughty goats and two beautiful peacocks happily doing what they do best: parading around and showing off their colourful feathers to ecstactic photographers.

It's hard to believe but some people come all the way here and miss entirely the magnificent temple located a hundred metres from the river... Just like a scene taken directly out of an Indiana Jones movie, a whole temple entangled in the roots of an immense tree, similar to what you see around Angkor wat, but not just partially covered but litterally swallowed. Only the door and the six windows are free from roots. The temple is not abandoned nor neglected, far from that... a queue of devotees are permanently walking in and out to pay respect to the golden Buddha seated inside the temple.

Amphawa is definitely the most attractive of all floating markets, having retained its authenticity and not yet on every tourist map. But Bangkokians love this place so much, that past noon it becomes impossible to walk. The best way to enjoy Amphawa is to come before 10:00 and leave soon after lunch.

Chinatown Bangkok

Bangkok's Chinatown is a popular tourist attraction and a food haven for new generation gourmands who flock here after sunset to explore the vibrant street-side cuisine. At day time, it's no less busy, as hordes of shoppers descend upon this 1-km strip and adjacent Charoenkrung Road to get a day's worth of staple, trade gold, or pay a visit to one of the Chinese temples.

Packed with market stalls, street-side restaurants and a dense concentration of gold shops, Chinatown is an experience not to miss. The energy that oozes from its endless rows of wooden shop-houses is plain contagious it will keep you wanting to come back for more. Plan your visit during major festivals, like Chinese New Year, and you will see Bangkok Chinatown at its best.

Best Restaurants in Bangkok Chinatown

If you are brave enough and forget everything you thought you knew about food, Chinatown will surprise you. Street food is always fun and travellers seem to enjoy mixing with locals to experience something traditional. Yaowarat is famous for its very popular food stalls balanced on the most impractical pavements, not to mention the dubious sanitary conditions. And yet, each plastic chair is occupied and a queue is patiently standing by, trying not to get hit by tuk tuks and bikes passing by.

There's also a small selection of indoor restaurants complete with menus in English, including the amazing Double Dogs tea room, with hundreds of types of tea, and Cotton at the stunning Shanghai Mansion where the food is a fusion of oriental flavours. Chinatown is adventure, and the sooner you discover it the better.

Lek & Rut Seafood in Chinatown

Bangkok is a city of extremes and this is particularly obvious when it comes to food. Here you can treat yourself to an extravagant and ludicrously expensive dinner on a rooftop restaurant, or eat a basic but excellent meal at a street stall for a handful of baht. Lek-Rut seafood in Chinatown is the most interesting mix of both culinary worlds, serving great food in the most unlikely surroundings you could dream of for a nice dinner: a frantic intersection of Bangkok Chinatown.

Apparently nothing differenciates Lek-Rut Seafood from its neighbouring street stalls, except that it is now famous, and of course popular. It's always packed and yet people patiently wait for a seat, standing wherever possible on the busy road. Don't expect tablecloth, silverware and air conditioning. In fact, don't even expect a restaurant! Set on the narrow sidewalk of the incredibly busy Yaowarat Road, it's a mystery how cars, bikes, by-passers manage to get past without hitting a dining table. Having diner at Lek-Rut is the perfect way to experience the way of life and culinary open-mind of Bangkok. You need to forget everything you know and just go with the flow, it's a fun and fascinating experience.

The staff are extremely efficient, very calm and friendly despite the crowd and the frenzy all around. Despite the anarchic appearances there is a logic, they are very good at remembering who came first in the crowd and you are taken to table in a matter of minutes. Once seated, the world around you suddenly shrinks to just your table and the food... Traffic noises, tuk tuk exhausts and whistling cops suddenly fade away as your full attention is drawn to the illustrated menu, which is in both Thai and in an approximate English, but consider yourself lucky, the translation is a little rough, and in some cases very amusing.

Lek Rut is an increasingly popular seafood restaurant in the heart of a big town and by street food standards it has become quite expensive, especially if you like big prawns, crabs and large fishes.

River prawns are massive and really delicious, grilled on request at the speed of light (or so it appears). Scallops stuffed with a bit of pork meat and bacon and grilled in their shells are definitely a must try, while cockles are popular among those who like this type of shells. The fried black crab in curry powder (between 350 and 500 baht according to size) is delicious if you are ready for a messy dinner: big black crabs shells are notoriously hard to break, but if you are not brave enough to fight with a crustacean, you can ask for just the crab meat. Their fish wrapped in pandanus leaves and cooked in foil is delightful (250 to 300 baht).

As mentioned earlier, for a street restaurant the price is high but it's also the most interesting experience... plastic stools, plastic plates on tin tables and toilet paper as tissue, tuk tuk noisily brushing you while cornering the intensely busy intersection of Yaowarat and Thanon Phadung Dao streets... and yet, once food is served nothing matters anymore. It's a surprisingly good dinner and we would happily go back and queue for more...

T & K Seafood

Serving delicious seafood, T & K restaurant (Toy and Kid are the names of the two brothers who own the place) on Yaowarat road is busy as a bee every single evening, come rain or shine. Just like many other popular restaurants in the area, it's not about fancy design and glamourous decor, but about great simple food and the rustic charm of eating on the pavement of a hectic street.

The outdoor area is the most popular but as it's permanently packed you can eat inside or even upstairs with air-con! Now if you associate air-con room with any kind of luxury you would be very wrong. The room is bare with the usual plastic chairs and iron tables, and the cleanliness applies no further than the top of your table, which by street food standards is all you need.

T & K is dedicated to seafood and once you tried their amazing whole fish served with different varieties of sauce either steamed or deep fried, huge barbecued prawns, crabs, a large array of great seafood soups, and best of all their delicious shells, then you will know why people queue up outside, even in the rain!

Location: Intersection of Yaowarat Road and Thanon Phadung Dao Street

Cotton Restaurant at Shanghai Mansion Hotel

Chinatown is certainly not short of eating establishments, but if you are looking to add a real touch of panache to your meal then it's impossible to beat the 1930s Shanghai parlour concept at Cotton restaurant. Located on the second floor of Shanghai Mansion Bangkok Boutique Hotel, the decor is simply wonderful, with a spiral cast-iron staircase, traditionally upholstered seating and period touches such as gramophones and antique furniture. The fact that Cotton restaurant faces onto Yaowarat Road means it is central to all the sites and shops of Chinatown and makes a great place for lunch or dinner.

An award winning chef is now at the helm of Cotton and under his stewardship they have compiled a tourist friendly menu that skirts its way through the best of Thai and Chinese cooking with a focus on taste and presentation:

To start we go for some crispy shrimp rolls (250 baht), which are rolled thin and long, and served poking out of a large wine glass. The shrimp is minced and plentiful inside, and the six 'sticks' per serving make a perfect appetiser when combined with the sweet, sticky dipping sauce. Next up we went for hot and sour Szechuan soup, packed with sea cucumber, shitake mushroom, egg, shrimp, and a special ingredient, sliced abalone (288 baht). The spice is definitely tempered for tourist palate but the sheer quantity of tastes and textures ensures it is a delicious option.

We followed this with a Chinese vegetarian dish, ma-po tofu (180 baht), and an interesting fusion creation of squid ink egg noodles with Chinese kale and crab claws (588 baht). The ma-po tofu is served with soft white tofu and a slightly tingling sauce it has the classic full flavour of the original but a little less oily than you would find in a Chinese restaurant. The crab claw dish was a real standout option: the claws are cracked with only the pincer shell remaining, meaning you get to enjoy the full flavour of the white flesh with the minimum of effort. When mixed with the thick stands of noodle and bitter vegetable with a slight crunch you have a recipe that delivers on taste and texture. The size of the dish means it can be enjoyed as a light lunch on its own or as a course during a longer dinner.

As well as excellent food, Cotton serves amazing cocktails and no visit is complete without trying a freshly muddled mojito or balanced martini, and dinner at Cotton has the added advantage of an excellent live band playing swing jazz every night from 21:00. The jazz band here is famed across Bangkok for a good time vibe.

If you are looking for a restaurant in Chinatown to deliver on style as well as substance, then Cotton should be your first stop.

Cotton Restaurant

Opening Hours: Lunch: 11:30 to 14:30 Dinner: 18:30 to 22:30
MRT: Hua Lamphong (short taxi or tuk tuk required)

Address: 479-481 Yaowaraj Road (Chinatown)

Tel: +66 (0) 2221 2121

Krua Porn Lamai

Krua Porn Lamai is a typical street food shack for those who enjoy eating like locals, and by that, we mean 'really local'. The dirty cooking station is on one side of the street while the tables on the other, lined against a sooty wall, so the waiters have to constantly cross the busy street with boiling hot plates. Despite its shabby appearance and just like most restaurants in Chinatown, Krua Porn Lamai is always full but for the first timer it takes a bit of courage to pick this place (don't expect an illustrated English menu, all you have is a short list written in Thai above the cart). Famous for its sizzling 'Hoi Tod' - mussels and soya beans omelet brought on a cast iron plate, and for its even more sizzling 'Radna'. Radna is a mix of prawns, squid, chicken and vegetables also brought on an iron dish, but here the cook will pour the gravy on the burning hot plate directly at your table, creating a bubbling smoky haze... it's as good as it's hot! Other recommended specialties are Kyua Taew Kua Krob - Stir fried crispy noodles and Taro Kua - Stir Fried Taro snacks (not the Taro root, but this is one of the only shop using this very popular fish strips snacks in place of noodles!).

Location: Soi Plang Nam, a street on the right hand side of Yaowarat road

Kuay Jab Nai Huan

Kuay Jab Nai Huan is one of Yaowarat road all time favourites... This small stall only serves one dish and is packed non-stop from six in the evening to late at night. Kuay Jab is made of large rolled rice noodles with crispy pork belly, sometimes with intestines and most importantly served in a very very peppery clear soup, with prices starting 40 baht. It's so popular you will certainly have to queue patiently, standing in this incredibly busy intersection, or if you are lucky, they might take you further down the lane to set a table up just for you, in the middle of nowhere.

Location: Intersection of Yaowarat Road and Yaowa Phanit streets

Odean Crab Noodle Soup

Odean is a very clean and rather discreet restaurant located behind Wat Traimit, in a small street near the Chinese gate of Odeon circle in Chinatown. Obviously it should have been called Odeon restaurant but it joined the many charming typos in Bangkok with the name 'Odean'. This is not just another noodle soup joint as a bowl can cost as much as 500 baht! The noodles are usually just traditional yellow egg noodles and the soup is light and clear... So what is their secret ingredient?

The key ingredient is nothing more than a delicious crab claw served on top of your soup... but not a tiny nipper... a big one, as big as you are willing to pay! So when ordering, you need to specify the price you wish to pay: from 200 to 500 baht. You can of course order a simple crab soup for 50 baht in which you will just get some crab meat, but the real deal here is to order a big claw. Everybody knows, the bigger, the better! You can also order the same dish but 'dry' where the soup itself is served separately.

Location: Charoen Krung Road, just near Wat Traimit and the big Chinatown red gate

Jok Kitchen

Jok Kitchen is without a doubt the best hidden restaurant in Bangkok, except for the fact that almost everyone in Bangkok has heard of it. But has everyone been there? probably not.

Despite its most unlikely location, it requires reservations weeks in advance; this is because Jok's Chinatown spot is also one on the smallest, most unusual and most talked about small restaurants in Bangkok: it can only accommodate 10 to 16 guests. To add to the mystery, you don't even get to choose the menu. All you need to know is that it's Thai-Chinese seafood and the Chef decides what's for dinner tonight. So there.... what is all the fuss about?

To get to Jok Kitchen, you better know how to get there - and once you actually find the street where the map took you somewhere in Chinatown, you still have to walk down a rather dark alley that smells of cat pee. At least four cats were sitting on now empty market stalls staring at us walking by. The narrow alley is a market at day and looks really abandoned at night. Further down, a sign, all in Thai, indicates an even smaller alley. I can imagine how a tourists coming to Bangkok for the first time would feel about this place... probably turn around and run for the closest KFC.

Once you've found it, the restaurant is not exactly impressive; small, white and brightly lit with neon lights with two large round tables so typical of Chinese restaurants. The whole set makes it pretty clear that you are here to enjoy food with friends and family, not the decorum.

The first dish soon arrives and all doubts are suddenly dissipated. The food is Thai-Chinese, simple and just like the restaurant, presented without unnecessary frills. First we were served a delicious light appetizer made of Ginko nuts with fried shallots on top, but the slices of abalone in a light wasabi sauce that followed was a real eye opener. The fried rice with crab meat with a smoky taste to it was the most simple yet hugely popular among my Thai friends. Fresh shrimp dumplings with deep fried garlic, one of the best snow fish I ever had (Gindara) on top of iceberg lettuce, big claws of four huge steamed crabs were the most expensive (6,000 baht). The weirdest dish if you are not yet familiar with is made of goose feet in glass noodle. Supposedly full of collagens.

Chef Jok is a humble and very friendly guy but you won't see him much unless you walk into his kitchen, which is as modest as his restaurant. Jok Kitchen without a doubt deserves his mysterious reputation of Bangkok's best hidden restaurant, reinforcing the fact the some of the best food ever served doesn't have to come with a cozy atmosphere and a convoluted plate decoration… it doesn't even have to be expensive!

Note that Chef Jok hinted us about a restaurant relocation. We suppose the place would be easier to find but if it were the case it might lose a bit of its 'hidden charm'. Whatever happens, we will go back as long as the food remains the same.

Jok Kitchen

Opening Hours: daily 11:30am - 2:30pm, 5:30 - 10pm
Location: Chinatown
Remarks: Reservation necessary
Address: 23 Soi Isara Nuphap, Phlab Phla Chai Road
Tel: 02-221-4075, 081-919-9468

Raan Look Khing and other sweets carts

No street dining experience in Chinatown would be complete without a fun local dessert. Often overlooked by travellers because of its unusual appearance, Thai sweets sold in the street bear no resemblance western desserts. Displayed on a tiny cart surrounded by the usual iron tables, small bowls are full of mostly unidentified multicoloured 'ingredients' used to prepare a cold dessert called 'Tao Tung'. You might recognize corn and red beans, but probably not the black jelly (Chao Kuai) or the green odd-looking noodles (Lod Chong), lotus, water chestnuts or the gingko nuts served in longan juice. You might even think this is a salad buffet!

Among the many sweets found along Yaowarat some are must-try: 'Bua Loy Num Khing' - rice balls stuffed with black sesame paste served in a very sweet and hot ginger sauce, or try 'Tao Tung Yen' - shaved ice with an assorted mix of the above mentioned toppings and covered with syrup, a great way to end a hot day or after a very spicy dinner. There are several of these carts along Yaowarat road, but Raan Look Khing (Baby Bamboo) at the intersection of Yaowarat road and Yaowa Phanit street is one of the most popular.

Location: Intersection of Yaowarat Road and Yaowa Phanit streets

Hua Seng Hong

One of Chinatown's more expensive options, but don't doubt that you will get your money's worth. This large restaurant is known for it extensive seafood menu, as well as an excellent dim sum assortment and more unusually, a good variety of sweet treats. There are set menus, or you can pick from an a la carte selection. We recommend the yellow curry with crab meat and the large sea bass with soy sauce which could easily feed 4 people. If you want one of the most raved about Thai desserts, try the crepe cake. The restaurant is clean and modern, a great place to enjoy Thai Chinese cuisine.

Opening Hours: 14:00 - 24:00
Address: 371-373 Yaowarat Road
Tel: +66 (0)2 222 0635

Himali Cha Cha

This long-established restaurant is the work of Cha Cha, who for 40 years cooked for the rich and famous. Cha Cha's son has maintained the family tradition of serving hearty Indian fare. Curries abound with mutton chutniwalla being the pick of the lot. Vindaloo is also recommended but for those of a less fiery disposition, chicken kashmiri, a rich, mild Himalayan blend with dried fruits, nuts and yoghurt will hit the spot. The restaurant is a chilled out spot in bustling Chinatown, with a lovely terrace and water feature outside. Inside they play soothing music and the service is swift and friendly.

Opening Hours: 10:00 - 23:00
Address: 1229/11 Charoen Krung (New Road) Soi 47/1
Tel: +66 (0)2 235 1569
Cuisine: Indian

Shopping in Chinatown

Shopping in Chinatown has a timeless quality to it and offers the perfect antidote to the modern mega-malls that are springing up in other areas of Bangkok. Here, tradition prevails and it possible to get lost down alleyways with traders selling the same specialist merchandise as their forefathers did generations ago. Prices are probably the cheapest you can find in the city, but bargaining is necessary and it can certainly get too hot and hectic for some, so we recommend taking it slow, stopping frequently to snack and drink, and enjoying the craziness of shopping in Chinatown with our Top 10 Guide.

Sampeng Lane Market

Sampeng Lane Market pretty much sums up the whole shopping experience of Chinatown and, to some extent, the surrounding Old City area; it's hot, busy, and the narrow lanes often become overly congested with vendors selling everything from fabrics, cheap clothes and electronics. As well as the steady flow of pedestrian traffic, pushcarts, worn-out vespers and the occasional truck overflowing with fresh produce all add to the madness.

But this definitely hectic nature of Sampeng is all part of the fun. Plus, this really is one of the cheapest places to come shopping in Bangkok, with impressive discounts available when you buy in bulk (10 or more items at a time gets you into wholesale territory). The most popular items to look out for are silk sarongs, jewellery, copied DVDs, women's shoes, home décor and appliances, kids' toys, cosmetics, handicrafts, dried food and all your usual tourist souvenirs.

The market, although usually known as just 'Sampeng', is actually located on Soi Wanit 1, a small alleyway running parallel to Chinatown's main Yaowarat Road. The shops and stalls aren't only restricted to this walkway though, with plenty more action to be found in the surrounding maze of sois. There's no particular layout at Sampeng meaning you'll probably get lost at some point, so set aside a good one or two hours to fully cover the area. Do note that this is not a night market, with most of the vendors packing up after sundown (around 18:00).

Naturally, food is another reason to visit this part of town. The main Yaowarat stretch is the best place to hit in the evening for a dinner, but there's plenty of great snacks to be had a Sampeng during the day like moo ping (barbequed pork), kanom buang (crispy tacos with sweet filling), mango and sticky rice, isaan sausage, fish cakes, spring rolls, rotis and ice cream (best tried it in a sandwich if you can find it). There's also a few guay diow (noodle soup) vendors that squeeze a few tables and chairs into a couple of dark, cramped nooks within the middle of Sampeng.

While street food, nightlife and temples will always entice tourists to the Old City and Chinatown, when it comes to shopping, Sampeng

Market is difficult to beat both in terms of price and fun... just as long as you're not in a rush nor mind working up a bit of a sweat

Sampeng Lane Market

Opening Hours: Daily 08:00:18:00
Location: Sampeng Lane, Soi Wanit 1, Chinatown, Bangkok

The Old Siam Plaza

The Old Siam Plaza on Burapha Road is a shopping mall in Bangkok's Old Town. Most of the indoor malls here are outdated but often brimming full of charm, and this is one such example. It's well-known throughout the local community for its two large open atriums packed with food vendors selling sweet and savoury treats, plus a standard selection of handicrafts, household appliances, and fashion.

We'd go as far as saying this is a 'hidden gem', but the substantial crowds streaming through the three-storey building every day would suggest otherwise. It's 'hidden' perhaps for the tourist market and Bangkok's younger generation, who normally stick to the convenience of Siam's megamalls.

So, what makes The Old Siam Plaza worth visiting? Apart from the nostalgic architecture, the answer is simple: the food! Most of the vendors here are located on the ground floor and the focus is all about traditional Thai deserts.

Now time for a quick Thai lesson. As you walk around, look out for kanom kuy chai (steamed dumplings), kanom sai sai (sweet coconut milk steamed in banana leaves), kanom buang (crispy pancakes with sweet stuffing), woon grob (Thai-style jelly with sugary topping), and kao tang savoey (sweet rice crackers). Those with less of a sweet tooth should look out for the excellent Chinese steamed buns (sala pao), with fillings such as bbq pork, chicken and salted egg.

There's reason to head upstairs too, with a good selection of silk and tailoring shops that cater for special events and ceremonies. This is also where you'll find a lot of the more generic items such as tourist souvenirs, handicrafts, and household appliances. On the far side of Old Siam Plaza there is also a whole section related to hunting and outdoor pursuits with everything from flashlights to camping gear and even firearms (which you need a license to purchase).

Old Siam Plaza is relatively easy to find on the corner of Burapha and Phahuratm Road, a short walk from the top of Yaowarat Road (Chinatown). Do note that there aren't too many ways to reach this part of town other than car/taxi, and traffic during morning and evening rush hours can be very bad (quieter from 10:00-15:00). Siam Old Plaza is open daily from 09:00-18:30.

The Old Siam Plaza

Opening Hours: 09:00-18:30

Location: The Old Siam Plaza, corner of Burapha Road and Phahuratm Road, Old Town Bangkok

Itsaraphap Lane

Itsaraphap Lane is a narrow, partially covered walking street which runs from the Chao Phraya River up to Leng Noi Yee Temple, the most important Chinese temple in Thailand. Along this street you will get a fascinating glimpse into everyday trading of all manner of dry goods: nuts, herbs, spices... and many more things you can only guess about! The most hectic stretch of Itsaraphap Lane is between Yaowarat and Leng Noi Yee Temple and is highly recommended. The cardboard cars, phones, and clothes are made especially for funerals so that family members might have them in the next life. For a great souvenir, we recommend buying some tea from around here.

Opening Hours: 09:00 - 18:00 (every day)
How to get there: The easiest way to find Itsaraphap Lane is to look for the large Tesco Lotus Supermarket on Yaowarat. The lane runs next to it up to Leng Noi Yee Temple.

Nightingale-Olympic: Bangkok's Strangest Mall

Bangkok has its fair share of strange stuff, a lot of which can be found in and around Chinatown. So then, it comes as little surprise that the capital's strangest and oldest shopping mall is only a short walk from the neighbourhood's main Yaowarat strip.

You'll instantly recognise the Nightingale-Olympic building, with its brutalist concrete façade towering above most of the other shophouses in the vicinity. We can only imagine how this must have appeared when it was unveiled as Bangkok's first ever department store 50 years ago, a time in which jungles and bamboo housing still covered vast suburban areas of the city.

Stepping foot inside, it becomes apparent that little has changed since Nightingale's grand opening in the early 1960s. The dilapidated atrium space is dimly lit, while the staff, who outnumbered me roughly 10 to 1, all have a rather despondent what-are-you-even-doing-here kind of look on their face.

Nightingale-Olympic almost feels like a living museum. You get the sense that the items on sale were once bought brand new, gradually becoming 'outdated' somewhere around the 90s and eventually evolving into the 'vintage-retro' category of today.

This means that there are actually a few great finds to be had, or at least gawped at. One highlight is a row of bizarre massage machines that lie you on your back with your feet up in the air, twirling them around unceremoniously. Incredibly, they're all still in working order - we're just not convinced about the therapeutic benefits.

There is an obvious focus on sports equipment and musical instruments, including cheesy tennis kits, rusty iron workout machines, a good range of guitars, drums, retro accordions and miniature pianos, foosball tables and miniature golf set still in the original packaging. Downstairs has a collection of cosmetic stalls, some manned by a few beauty therapists who like they've been in the same job for decades, which they probably have.

As Bangkok's first ever department store, this really was the Siam Paragon or EmQuartier of its day. It was a pioneer of the capital's emerging retail scene, with over 100 staff employed across several more floors. As well as being Bangkok's oldest shopping centre, Nightingales surely wins the title of 'the strangest' simply because we don't know how it has stayed open this long.

Find Nightingale-Olympic just on Triphet Kwang Road, close to the corner with Pahurat Road. Do note the building's no-photos rule, which as you can see, is not very well enforced.

Nightingale-Olympic

Opening Hours: 09:00 - 18:00 (closed Sundays)
Address: 70 Triphet Khwang Wang Road, just off of Pahurat Road
Tel: +66 (0)2 221 9773

Flashlight Market (Khlong Thom)

Best known for secondhand goods and assorted knick-knacks, Klong Thom Market sees action every Saturday from 17:00 onwards, and continues going until Sunday's early evening. Formerly known as

'Flashlight Market' due to the fact that buyers will need a flashlight to see the goods, this market is especially crowded on late Saturday night. Covering areas of Luang, Worachak and Charoenkrung, Suar Pa Roads, Klong Thom has everything from car spare parts, DVDs and CDs, electronic devices to clothing items and toys. Besides the roadside stalls, there's also a three-storey Klong Thom Centre (close to Worachak Road) where car accessories and toys are on sale. If you want to avoid the crowd, best time to go is Sunday morning from 8:00 until 11.00.

Opening Hours: Saturday 17:00 until Sunday 17:00 (a few traders open every day)
Location: corner of Worachak Road and Chao Kamrop Road

Little India Bangkok

Little India in Bangkok, known locally as 'Phahurat Market', is just a short walk from the city's famous Chinatown, not too far away from the banks of the Chao Phraya River.

And its label of 'little' is certainly appropriate; the neighbourhood is made up of just one short road with only a few giveaways that it is home to Bangkok's largest Indian community, such as a prominent golden-domed Sikh temple, some shabby (but very delicious) curry houses and lots of traditional textile shops.

Eating in Little India

Indian food may actually be the neighbourhood's main draw for the first-time tourist, who has more than enough sights, sounds and smells to get to grips with over on the much more popular Yaowarat Road (Chinatown). A quick detour to Phahurat Road uncovers a few curry-house gems that go big on authentic flavour, and less about the décor and general cleanliness. This might put off the squeamish, but do remember you'll be paying about 100 baht for a place of curry, rice and a naan bread about a quarter of what it costs over in Sukhumvit.

Restaurants to look out for include Royal India (392/1 Th Chakraphet), and Toney Restaurant (64/1 Soi Rimklongongarg), although sometimes it's just best to get yourself lost in the maze of sois surrounding Phahurat Road and find a spot that seems right for you

Sights

By far the most prominent attraction in Little India Bangkok is Sri Guru Singh Sabah Temple. Built in 1932 for many of the northwestern Indian Sikhs who migrated to Thailand at the turn of the 20th century, this is actually the second largest Sikh temple outside of India. The giant building, topped off with golden domes rising above Bangkok's busy streets, really defines the area and is difficult to miss. Most choose to admire the temple from the outside, although everybody is welcome to take a look around, and they even serve up a free vegetarian breakfast (2nd floor) every morning.

Phahurat Shopping

Unsurprisingly, textile, fabric and traditional dress shops make up the majority of shopping options in Bangkok's Little India. There is also a four-storey mall here which many consider to be the centre of Little India known as 'India Emporium'. Inside this rundown mall the fabrics theme continues, with many dress shops specializing in custom-made garments for special occasions. You can also purchase silk of all different types and colours by the square metre. Other items to look out for are second-hand electronics, Bollywood-themed DVDs and CDs, jewellery, dried spices and Hindu/Sikh artwork.

Find Little India in Bangkok on Phahurat Road, five minutes' walk from Chinatown (Yaowarat Road). The nearest MRT Station is Hua Lamphong, around 5-10 minutes taxi or tuk-tuk drive away (depending on traffic).

Little India (Phahurat)

Location: Little India Bangkok, Phahurat Road

Saphan Lek Market

It is thought that certain customs duties haven't been paid on most of the items here, and therefore bargain hunters can save up to 40% off department store prices. Bootleg software, pirated videos, unlicensed cassette tapes; these are just some of the things that you can find crammed into the aisles that make up Bangkok's Talat Saphan Lek. Just to the west of Chinatown, The 200-metre-long aisles, which run along both banks of the canal, stretch from Charoen Krung or New Road south to Yaowarat Rd.

Opening Hours: 09:00 18:00
Location: Iron Bridge Market. The market itself is built on a large metal bridge over Ohng Ang Canal in the Wang Burapha

Bangkok Museums

Bangkok's many museums exhibit some of the most sublime, and strangest, collections of relics you can imagine, giving visitors a wonderful insight into Thailand's colourful culture and unique heritage. Some are housed in buildings just as interesting as their contents, like Kamthieng House, a 19th Century teak house and former abode of a rice farmer, the Bangkok Folk Museum and Jim Thompson's House. The best place to start has to be the National Museum, in Rattanakosin. Its collections spanning all periods of Thai history offer an unsurpassed introduction to the country's art and architecture. Be sure to allow enough time for your visit, as it is very easy to get lost in a time that is long gone.

Bangkok National Museum

In the former grounds of the 18th Century Wang Na Palace, The Bangkok National Museum houses the largest collection of Thai art and artifacts in the country. It's definitely worth a visit, especially if visiting nearby Wat Phra Kaew or the Grand Palace.

Opened by King Rama V to exhibit the antiques and gifts bestowed to him by his father, it once held a reputation for being an ill-organised gathering of dusty relics. That has now changed, with exhibits now arranged into three areas consistent with Thai history, and good English-language descriptions available.

The front of the Sivamokhaphiman Hall is a Thai history gallery spanning the Sukothai through to the Rattanakosin periods. The Archaeological and Art History collection showcases items from Thailand's prehistory to Sukhotahai and Ayutthaya eras right through to the modern Thai Kingdom, including many ancient sculptures.

Among scores of interesting collections in the decorative arts and ethnological collection are Chinese weapons, gold treasures, precious stones, Khon masks, puppets, ceramics, clothing and textiles, woodcarving and traditional musical instruments from around Southeast Asia.

Other exhibits of interest at the Bangkok Nationla Museum include a funeral chariot hall, featuring carriages used for royal cremations, and many excellent examples of Thai architecture. These include the Buddhaisawan chapel, a teak or 'red' house called Tam Nak Deang and various beautiful pavilions. Free English-language tours given by volunteers are available and also conducted in German (Thursdays), French and Japanese (Wednesdays).

Bangkok National Museum

Opening Hours: 09:00 - 16:00 (Wednesday - Sunday)
Location: Na Phrothat Road, near the Grand Palace
Tel: +66 (0)2 215 8173
How to get there: Taxi is probably the best way to go. Or embark the Chao Phraya Express Boat to Maharaj Pier, then walk about 20 minutes.

Museum of Siam

While the Museum of Siam is set inside a very large neoclassical house, it is definitely not the usual display of historical artifacts and dusty mannequins you would expect to find in such an antique building.

A huge bronze 'ribbon' coiling and looping in the front garden is the first clue of things to come inside... In the reception area, wooden stairs, ceramic tiles and old-fashioned columns contrast with resolutely modern art and advanced technology. Everywhere you look, the two elements blend with great harmony as designers use every possible way to challenge the traditional expectations you might have of a museum.

In the reception area, the bronze ribbon seen outside almost seems to penetrate the building and curls from wall to wall with the words 'What does being Thai mean?' written in red luminous letters all along. The entire museum is dedicated to this 'Thainess', the history of Thai people and the evolution of their culture and traditions.

It is extremely well done. Once you enter the first room the giant ribbon called 'The Roong' seems to have crossed the wall to become a long panoramic screen on which you will be asked to watch a movie. This movie will immerse you through artistic and sometimes provocative images into the Thai spirit. Never boring and beautifully executed, it will wipe out your last doubts about the museum. After only 10 intense minutes, you are mentally ready to appreciate the many other surprises of the Museum of Siam

From room to room, 'The Roong' transports you through all things Thai, from the very beginning of Ayutthaya to the daily life and highlights of Thai history, wars, Buddhism and finally the rapid entry into the modern world. Every room is superbly decorated and time will pass faster than you expect, with many interactive displays.

If the first part of the Museum of Siam exhibit appears to be a bit 'classic' things start to change when Thailand started adopting Western ideas. From there on, the exposition becomes even more surprising: walk through spirals or TV screens broadcasting the evolution of Thai TV programs through the years, then step into a fancy 'Bangkok Café' from the sixties where you can actually sit or get behind the counter. Teenagers can't resist taking photos of each other in this colourful room with half a car parked in front, but obviously no drinks will be served.

Once outside, don't go yet; take a walk over to that strange small shop near the souvenir boutique. At first it looks like some entrepreneur has managed to sneak his local shop into the museum and it's a bit awkward to walk around looking at pickles and fish sauce bottles. But the girl shopkeeper will solve the mystery for you; it's all part of the exhibit. Here are all the daily ingredients made in Thailand yesterday and still today, how they were made and why they were made. And suddenly you start looking at fermented beans with a new mindset.

So as you are about to leave the 'shop' the girl will call you and invite you to step inside her fridge. At this point you might consider running or laughing. Step in! This is actually the entrance to the next (and last) display a full-size European restaurant with chandelier and real waitresses. Nothing to eat here, just enjoy the wax displays of many Thai dishes and have fun taking lots of photos.

Museum of Siam Bangkok

The Museum of Siam is a surprising exhibition, and even if museums are usually not part of your holidays, it's a great introduction to Thailand's spirit and culture without ever being boring. And as it's located not far from Wat Pho, it a nice addition to a day trip in this part of Bangkok.

Opening Hours: 10.00 - 18.00 (Tuesday to Sunday)
Location: Phra Nakorn District, Rattanakosin Island, south of Wat Pho
Tel: +66 (0)2 225 2777

Moca - Museum of Contemporary Art Bangkok

A must for any lover of art, the Museum of Contemporary Art in Bangkok (MOCA) houses the most comprehensive collection of modern painting and sculpture in Thailand inside a striking, purpose built gallery. The five storeys of MOCA contain over 800 pieces of art collected by communications magnate Boonchai Bencharongkul and showcase the development of Thai fine art since the introduction of modern western concepts. The museum is open from 10:00 to 18:00, Tuesday to Sunday (closed on Monday), and costs 180 baht for the general public. It costs 80 baht for students and for visitors over the age of 60 or under 15, admission is free.

MOCA is everything a world class art gallery should be: thought provoking, beautiful and, in parts, funny. Thailand has, at times, been criticised for 'sugar coating' many of the social issues that the country faces, and that is why MOCA is so refreshing: a place where artists are free to explore themes such as religion, corruption, prostitution and the loss of traditional values. All of Thailand's National Artist recipients have pieces on display and although you could whizz through the gallery in a couple of hours, to really experience it we recommend spending up to four hours here.

Built in 2012, MOCA has been specifically designed to give guests the best possible conditions for appreciating the art on show. Lots of natural light and well spaced rooms ensure this art gallery is equal to any abroad. There is a coffee shop on the ground floor serving Twinings tea, hot chocolate and coffee from the Royal Patronage Project which tries to promote fair trade and sustainability. However, the food on offer is severely lacking with only pre-packed sandwiches and biscuits for sale.

While Thailand is renowned for its traditions and culture, there have been few art galleries of international standard to showcase the growing number of world class Thai artists. The Museum Of Contemporary Art in Bangkok is now providing a space in which to display the best of Thai art for everyone to enjoy.

Artists to Look Out For

Prateep Khotchabua's art is striking, both for its bold use of colour and playful, sometimes surrealist scenes. Animalism and nudity is a prominent theme in several of his works, sometimes with one animal morphing into another. However, I most enjoyed his work Luang Ta Ma (Traditional Thai Music), 2002, which is a portrait of a rural family cavorting by the riverside. The attention to detail is fantastic and every family member is present and enjoying a facet of Thai life that is today in decline or already gone. Young boys can be seen catching shrimp in the river while up on the pavilion men sit around a jar betting on a fish fight; cats, dogs and chickens are scampering here and there and the whole scene seems boisterous yet full of a sense of community.

Chalermchai Kositpipat, designer of the famous all-white temple (Wat Rong Khun) in Chiang Rai province, has several of his paintings on permanent display at MOCA. Combining Buddhist themes with a traditional Thai style, he explores the relevance of Buddhism even in today's urban environment. There is a vibrant pointillist style painting on the second floor by Preecha Pun-Klum entitled Glamourous Night in Bangkok, 2009, that captures the hectic energy of Bangkok by night, and on the fourth floor, three gigantic paintings depict The Three Kingdoms Heaven, Earth and Hell with astounding attention to detail.

On the fifth floor is a special wing dedicated to European painters from the Victorian era, with many fine period pieces, as well as an ensemble of Vietnamese, Chinese, Italian and Japanese artwork. You will also find rooms dedicated to the lifetime achievements of two of Thailand's most revered artists Chalood Nimsamer, who uses the recurring image of his daughter to represent peace, warmth and gentleness, and the late Paitun Muangsomboon (d.1999) who was a central figure in the progression of sculpture from that of ideals to that of hyper-realism both of whom are regarded as National Artists in Sculpture.

MOCA

Opening Hours: 10:00 18:00, Tuesday to Sunday (Closed on Monday)
Location: MOCA is only reachable by taxi. The five storey building is easy to spot from Vibhavadi Road, but the taxi must go past the museum and make a U-turn on Changwattana Road, travelling back down a small road beside the train tracks.
BTS: Mo Chit (still requires a 10 minute taxi journey)
Address: 3 Vibhavadi Rangsit, Chatuchak, Bangkok
Tel: +66 (0) 2953 1005
Price Range: 180 baht Student: 80 baht children/OAP: Free

Bangkokian Museum

The Bangkokian Museum in Bangrak is hard to find and is not even very well known. It's a simple, discreet museum but the charm is in the pleasure of discovering this small frozen-in-time gem. In fact the Bangkokian museum, sometimes called 'Bangkok Folk Museum', consists mostly of two beautiful wooden houses preserved in perfect condition just the way they were last century.

Set in a tiny street not far from River City and the famous Oriental Hotel, the houses stand in the back of a garden, behind a large wooden gate, and despite the large signboard 'Bangkokian Museum', it is really easy to miss.

Walk into the garden to the reception counter and just write down your name inside the guest book: yes, entry is free! Depending who is on duty that day, you will hear a very short explanation in approximate English or a well-described story from the lady owner.

The first house is the largest and more beautiful one, with immaculately varnished flooring and green painted wooden walls. The ground floor includes the dining rooms, offices and library, while upstairs are the bedrooms with their cute very old fashion en-suite bathrooms. Every room has original Bakelite switches, antique standing clocks, massive valve radios and cabinets with encrusted nacre. Daily objects are kept inside antique closets and if it was not for few glass boxes displaying some of the most valuable items, you would almost expect the master of the house to step into the room and slip into one of the beds after washing his face in the old-fashioned porcelain basins.

The breeze flowing through keeps this two-storey house nice and comfortable without need of fans. All the rooms are very tiny but the veranda in the back is large so it is easy to imagine people spending most of their time in the garden, in the shade of the huge trees. Despite being in a very busy area of Bangkok, this garden is a haven of total peace.

A bit behind the main building is a second, smaller house, originally built in the countryside, deconstructed and reassembled here in

Bangkok. The style is clearly different: almost all walls, floors and ceilings are made of dark reddish teakwood and features a lot more windows and less wall space. The ground floor appears to be a small dining area and office and the upper floor is a large bedroom with a spotlessly waxed floor. Here too, everything is set to welcome guests and the bed is made. The idea to try it is very tempting.

Next to the two classic houses is a larger, and more recent building used as a museum of eclectic objects collected at any given time in the past, most of them without apparent historical value, and some even appear to be very recent. Upstairs is a gallery of photos taken around Bangkok and Thailand in the past centuries.

The Bangkokian Museum is more of a charming stop than a real museum visit. But if you happen to explore this part of Bangkok riverside, it's well worth it and makes a nice photo opportunity, especially if you have been to Bangkok several times before and are looking for something off the beaten track.

Bangkokian Museum

Opening Hours: 10:00 - 16:00, Wednesday to Sunday
Location: 73 Charoen Krung, turn into the small soi 43 and pass under the bridge, then look on your right
Tel: 02 234 6741
Price Range: Free

Vimanmek Mansion in Bangkok

Vimanmek Royal Mansion is currently closed for renovation

Located on Ratchawithi Road behind the National Assembly, Vimanmek Royal Mansion is the world's largest building made entirely of golden teak. Removed from Ko Sichang in Chonburi province, it was rebuilt in the Dusit Palace in 1900 by the command of King Rama V. It was recently renovated by HM Queen Sirikit, and made into a museum paying homage to the late King.

As well as antique furniture, there's glassware, porcelain, old photographs and memorabilia from the late King's reign (1868 - 1910). Many rooms currently maintain the atmosphere of the past.

A guided tour is provided to visitors. Most of the building in the same compound are now used as museums. The outstanding one is Abhisek Dusit Hall, which exhibits HM Queen Sirikit's collection of handicraft masterpieces created by rural people. The other displays of various items and art objects including HM King Bhumibol's photography, paraphernalia of rank and portraits, ancient cloth, clocks, and royal carriages. Parts of Vimanmek are still used for various state functions and receptions for visiting royalty when the buildings are closed to the public. Traditional Thai dancing commences daily at 10:30 and 14:00.

Vimanmek Mansion

Opening Hours: 08:30 until 16:30 (Tuesday - Saturday, last ticket at 15:30)
Location: Rajavithee Road. Close to Dusit Zoo and the Dusit Palace complex.

Price Range: 100 baht, which entitles you to enter every building and gallery. Note that you will need to show your ticket to the attendant at the entrance to every building. Please note: No shorts or sleeveless shirts and skirts must be at least knee-length or you won't be allowed in.

The End

9 781715 758479